From Rags to... More Rags

Two Friends, $200 and a Multimillion Dollar Cleaning Business

David W. Murphy and Gary L. Collins
Co-Founders of Supreme Maintenance Organization

Table of Contents

Foreword

The first time I remember meeting David Murphy and Gary Collins was in the fifth grade playing dodgeball on the playground at Joyner Elementary School in Greensboro, North Carolina. The way I remember them, David was a pretty decent athlete and Gary was a little on the small side. Truth be told, they were both "scrubs." You see, I can get by with calling them that because we're great friends and because I went on to become a Division 1 basketball player at James Madison University (JMU). In fact, nowadays when David introduces me to one of his friends, he loves to tell them that my claim to fame is that I once held David Robinson, The Admiral, to 50 points when my JMU Dukes played his nationally ranked Navy team. I always quickly respond that I, however, scored 18 points on Robinson. The truth is that Robinson actually scored 45 points and tied a Navy record while only playing 32 minutes due to foul trouble, and I scored 13 points.

Anyway, back in our school days, I remember my class competing against David and Gary's class in different activities, and of course my class would always win. Gary seemed to be a well-mannered, nice guy and David had more of a swagger and attitude. Little did I know that these two "scrubs" would go on to start and build the largest janitorial service based in Greensboro, and that we would become such long-lasting friends.

My relationships with David and Gary started to blossom in seventh grade when we played on the JV football team at the then Aycock Middle School. Each and every year we became closer and closer, whether it was having classes together or sharing the same interests. In high school, David and I played football at Page High School and competed for State 4A Championships while Gary was the smart one and had a job (and the girls). During our college days, me at JMU, David at UNC, and Gary at Elon, we did not stay in touch as much, but shortly after college we connected again as we all embarked on our careers. David and Gary had launched Supreme Maintenance Organization (SMO) in 1989, and I was a college basketball coach at Wingate College and UNCG, and later started my real estate career.

During my coaching days, I would come home and help Gary and David with their cleaning jobs during my summers off. We would perform construction clean-up jobs and I helped them clean a few post offices. We would sometimes hang out at their tiny 300 square foot office on 4th Street, just off of Summit Avenue. I reflected back to my days growing up in Woodmere Park, when every day I would pass by the Phillips Avenue office of Murphy Services, the janitorial service business owned by David's father. I thought that since the janitorial service was in David's blood and Gary was such a nice, hard-working guy, their business would be successful. I believe having fathers with tremendous work ethics is one of the commonalities that the three of us share. Over the years we have all three focused on our Christian faith, family and work.

Of course, we also could still find ways to have fun. One of my most memorable times during SMO's formative years was when we all took a road trip in David's dad's conversion van to Atlanta. (THIS WAS BEFORE WE WERE MARRIED OR HAD ANY KIDS!) We had food and refreshments on the way down as we watched TV and played video games. While in Atlanta we went so see our old high school teammate, Haywood Jeffries, who was an All-Pro receiver for the Houston Oilers, take on the Atlanta Falcons. After the game we had the opportunity to visit our friends, and we met a nice cab driver that took us to a few prime locations for nightlife activities. I don't remember all the details of that night, but I do remember it came at a really good time because Gary and David were working extremely hard and were under a lot of pressure. I was a little surprised they were both able to take some time off, but it was an opportunity to blow off some steam.

Throughout the years, Gary, David and I have enjoyed spending time together watching college football or other sporting events. These events are usually accompanied by family and great food. David and Gary are both diehard Carolina Tar Heel football fans and even support Carolina Athletics through the Ram's Club. I love harassing them about Carolina football and the team's inconsistency and lack of success over the years. I can get David fired up pretty quickly when I start talking junk about Carolina football. Of course, basketball is an entirely different story.

I have really enjoyed watching Gary and David grow SMO to a company with over 600 employees while still maintaining a family environment. Longevity of employees is a vital characteristic of a successful business, and SMO has many. Their employees reflect the work ethic, moral values and dedication that Gary and David live by every day. I have personally witnessed many times in which the company has gone beyond the call of duty to help out their employees.

Gary and David have two totally different personalities but share the same core beliefs: faith, family and integrity. I'm truly blessed to call them both friends. As you go through life you can consider yourself lucky if you have just one true friend that you can count on if you only had one call to make. With Gary and David, I'm blessed to have two such friends that I could call on in a time of need, as I did in 2010.

As you might imagine, my real estate business suffered greatly after the real estate crash of 2008. In 2010 I decided to start my own cleaning business, NewWay Building Services, to help supplement my lost income and support my family. Gary and David were instrumental in helping me get started and even allowed me to subcontract several of their smaller cleaning accounts. In developing a partnership with SMO and working closely with Gary and David, I got a close-up view of two God-fearing men running a company the same way they lived their life, with high morals, integrity and a strong work ethic.

Throughout their thirty years at SMO, Gary and David have experienced many ups and downs. I know there have been many times they've felt like giving up, but they have continued to persevere. They have proven that when the going gets tough, the tough continue to strive for better. Even though they've reached a milestone of 30 years of service, they continue to strive to make SMO better every day. I look forward to their continued success, and more Carolina football arguments.

As you read this story of two average guys from O' Henry Oaks in Greensboro who took $200 and mom's vacuum and turned it into a growing, multimillion-dollar janitorial business, I hope you are inspired to go out and achieve your dreams. As David and Gary will tell you, you don't have to have a new Internet startup or a great invention to build a successful business. Faith, hard work and grit can carry you a long way toward reaching your goals. Although they may never be high tech billionaires, Gary and David's story is a true rags to riches story, or should I say rags to...more rags. Enjoy!

John E. Newman Jr.
Broker/Realtor
John Newman Realty

Acknowledgements

We have so many people to thank because we certainly could never have achieved any of the success of Supreme Maintenance Organization, or had a book to write about it, on our own. We would like to start by thanking our Lord and Savior, Jesus Christ. Without His guiding hand, SMO would simply not be. We would also like to thank our wives, Lisa Collins and Paula Murphy, who have supported our little venture from the very beginning. They put up with all the long hours and not having us around, especially during those early "manure" days—those long, difficult days required to grow a startup business with no start-up capital. We could not ask for more supportive wives. Of course, we would also like to recognize our children, Chris, Sarah (now Sarah King) and Kevin Collins, and Melanie, Michelle, Mark and Montana Murphy for allowing us the opportunity to be dads during this wild ride. All of our children have worked for SMO at some point in one capacity or another and we could not imagine this journey without them.

We would like to thank our parents, the late Jimmy Murphy, who started his janitorial business, Murphy Services, back in the 1960s and taught us so much about the business. We doubt that SMO would have ever gotten started without Mr. Murphy. We also would like to thank

David's mother, Faye Murphy, for letting us set up shop in her spare bedroom. Gary would especially like to thank Mrs. Murphy for not accepting David's offer to be his partner, clearing the way for his involvement. We are also very grateful to Gary's parents, Paul and Louise Collins, for allowing us to use their computer and dot matrix printer and, more importantly, for a bailout loan to get us out of trouble with the IRS. We would also like to thank them for teaching Gary the tremendous work ethic that has served him so well all these years.

We have several friends that really helped us out in those early days. We need to start with Fred Joseph, who was a Greensboro insurance executive and part of the football coaching staff with David at Page High School. Mr. Joseph, or "Mr. J." as we referred to him, assisted us with our first buy/sell agreement, and he was critical in helping us establish accounting and banking relationships. He also helped us land a contract to clean a building owned by him and his partners.

We have several friends who worked with us helping to clean during those early days, when it was so important to be able to hire people we could trust. We would like to thank Anthony "Roni" Oliver, Addison "Mocking Up Duh Flo" Edwards, Babette Weaver Smith, who also starred in our first advertisement photo, and John E. Newman, Jr., who also contributed to this book by writing the Foreword. We would also like to thank Ken Allen, who grew up in our neighborhood right across the street from Gary, for helping us out with a few of those early construction clean-up jobs. Ken is currently SMO's Corporate Controller, helping us manage all aspects of our finances. We often tell people that Ken cares more about our money than we do. We are not sure if we could have made it through those difficult days without them.

We would like to thank David's sisters, Sherrie Cummins and Dale Sharp, who at different times both worked for us part-time as a bookkeeper. Sherrie also helped us win a cleaning contract for a local dental office when she was their office manager, and Dale motivated David by telling him how crazy he was to work all those long hours cleaning toilets since he had a college degree from UNC. Once again, it was nice to have someone in that critical position that we knew we could trust.

We also would like to recognize a few early key customers who were willing to give two young inexperienced kids a chance. The late Mike Davidson, who was the Facility Manager at the Kmart Distribution Center, gave us our first big break by hiring two 20-something-year-olds to clean a 1.6 million square foot facility. Mike will always have a special place in the history and success of SMO. Allen Lillard, the Senior Facility Manager for Starmount Company, a leading property management company in Greensboro, gave us an opportunity to clean all their commercial office buildings along the very prestigious Green Valley Road in 1997. Although Mr. Lillard has since retired, SMO is still serving this customer who now operates under a new name. We would also like to thank Ron F., who was a church friend of Gary's, for helping us get started with a logistics customer back in 1998 and is today our largest customer with almost 100 locations served. This customer addition came at a very crucial time, as we had just lost our largest customer.

We would also like to thank all of our current customers for entrusting SMO to serve their cleaning needs. We are very blessed to have the opportunity to work with some of the best businesses and organizations in the Southeast. This has given us the opportunity to develop some long-term partnerships with some really fine folks.

We would also like to thank our Peer Group members who have contributed to this book: Val and Steve Garcia, Tiffany and Terry Woodley, Jim and Bob Armbruster, and Marcell Haywood. We would not be where we are today without the support and encouragement that you guys have given to us over the years.

We have hundreds of valued SMO team members that we would like to thank, but because it would not be practical to list them all here we would like to recognize those that have served with us for over 20 years: Diana Wilson, VP of Business Development; Al Summers, District Manager; Duryea "Juice" Taylor, Quality Assurance Manager; Jesus Fonseca, Account Manager; Steve Gardner, Trainer; Marlene Lash, Leroy "Rookie" Haywood, Paul Cathcart and Etta Tweedy. We cannot leave out Shanda

Everett, Office Manager, who doesn't quite have 20 years but is the glue that holds the SMO office together.

We are sure we are leaving out some important individuals and we hope that you will accept our sincere apologies. We don't know for sure where this journey will end up taking us, but we do know that we could not have gotten this far without all those who have helped us along the way. Once again, we say a very heartfelt THANK YOU.

Introduction

Thirty years ago, nobody could have told us, David Murphy and Gary Collins, that we would write a book about our business someday. No way! Back in 1989, we were just a couple of young guys knocking on doors in Greensboro, North Carolina trying to get a janitorial business off the ground. Launching a business on an initial investment of $100 apiece and a borrowed Kenmore canister vacuum cleaner, you wouldn't exactly say we got off to a running start.

In those early days, we did all the cleaning ourselves, sometimes starting in the early morning and not finishing until…early the next morning. Almost everyone we knew told us we would never make our business work, that we should get out now and find ourselves a real career. There were many late-night moments when one or both of us were inclined to agree.

Yet here we are, celebrating our 30th year as co-founders of Supreme Maintenance Organization. Our little business has grown up into a multi-million-dollar operation servicing a wide spectrum of office complexes, schools, and industrial facilities throughout North Carolina, South Carolina and Virginia. We've climbed to the top three percent of our industry nationwide in terms of revenue. Instead of worrying about whether we should pack up our rags and get out, we're firmly setting our sights on new goals for the future.

Yep, we've mopped and scrubbed our way to a long-term successful business. Now it's our time to stop for a moment to take a breath and chronicle our journey.

Of course, we're the first to admit that we're not all that special or unique. Lots of small businesses have started with nothing and reached great heights, especially in the janitorial service industry. We're just two guys too determined or too stubborn to quit that managed to support our families and provide employment for more than 600 employees, with a story that we have been told many times is a real "wow." So we're telling that story now. In a time when half of all small businesses fail within the first few years, we've endured over three decades and kept steadily marching ahead. The two of us have done this together, bolstered by a partnership that looks a lot like a marriage when you consider all the time we spend together and all the decisions we have to mutually agree on. Not many marriages last 30 years these days, and most business partnerships sure don't hold together that long, so we've managed to stand the test of time.

We're putting together the history of SMO first for our kids and grandkids before we get too old to remember it. We also offer it to anyone who may be just starting out or planning to launch a cleaning business, or any other small business. As you read this book, we hope that you will discover a few messages that you'll find helpful in striving to reach your entrepreneurial dreams.

For one thing, we can assure you that even if you were not the brightest student in your class, and you were not born with a silver spoon in your mouth, you can still start your own business and, through hard work, good decision-making and a spirit of never quitting, you too can achieve satisfying success. Our example may also serve as a reminder that when you're deciding what kind of business to go into, you don't need to have some new idea, a creative invention or some pioneering, earth-shattering technique or philosophy about whatever it is you're doing. That approach may work for some people, but it is not the only way to build a successful business.

We're also writing this book as our way to honor the cleaning service industry. For some people, the stigma of being "just a janitor" still lingers, but we're here to assure you that those women and men who clean your offices, your stores, your banks and your schools are some of the best, most humble people you could ever know. Like us, some of them have built a highly successful cleaning business. Because we believe that more of their stories should be known and appreciated, we have included profiles of four other very successful janitorial services in this book.

We may not be experts on steering a book around one major theme, but we did come up with a few key ideas that you will see highlighted in the chapters ahead:

• **Partnership** - You're going to go through all kinds of trials and tribulations in running a small business, especially in non-glamorous industries like ours, and you'll be much better off doing it with someone you really know and can deeply trust. Just as the close bonds of good teammates can help a football or baseball team win a championship, a solid business partnership can bolster your chances of achieving the kind of success you envision. With the right partner (and as we will explain later, it's critical that you don't try to fly with the wrong partner!), you can always be confident that when the chips are down, somebody's got your back.

• **Perseverance** - It was Jim Valvano from our state of North Carolina who made popular that phrase "Don't give up, don't ever give up." As we discovered, that commitment not to quit self-perpetuates itself over time. When you face one challenge or difficulty and keep pushing until you get over the hump, it gives you more confidence and momentum to rise up and successfully meet the next obstacle. Like us, you may find that you need others to remind you that you've got to hold tightly to your commitment when the storm clouds circle overhead. When their voice speaks, listen to it. You must have grit and determination to build a successful business from nothing.

• **People** - Any business that relies on men and women to perform a service that many would never take on, and often do their work alone on "the island" inside an empty building late at night, must have great people to succeed. We've been blessed to have hundreds of really good people, some of whom have stayed with us for 10, 15 or even 20-plus years. We're not foolish enough to believe that when someone on our team is successful, it's all because of our great leadership or excellent training. It's because of who our people are—their caring attitude and the spirit of service they bring to this job. To the dedicated team members of SMO, this celebration is really about you!

Well, that's enough warm-up talk. Time to flip the switch and present to you our story of 30 years of building and growing Supreme Maintenance Organization. Thanks for tuning in!

CHAPTER 1

Roots of a Partnership

When did our partnership begin? Well, you could say that it started when we launched Supreme Maintenance Organization together in 1989. But that doesn't tell the whole story of how two C students from Greensboro, North Carolina happened to get together and build a multimillion-dollar janitorial service. No, if you really want to track the roots of our successful and enduring partnership as co-founders of SMO, you've got to turn the clock back a lot longer than 30 years.

You need to back it up at least as far as those nights when we were teenagers, when we would sit for hours under the street light on the corner of Sandburg Drive and Guest Street in Greensboro until 1 or 2 a.m., just chewing tobacco and talking about sports and girls and other things two adolescent boys might choose to discuss at that hour. Maybe you even have to look earlier than that, starting around five or six years after we were born a couple of months apart in 1965.

David lived a few houses up on the left from our favorite street corner on Sandburg Drive, and Gary lived a few houses down on the right on Guest Street, just a block off Summit Avenue and Yanceyville Street. It was the kind of neighborhood where the simple houses had to rely on window

Corner of Guest Street & Sandburg Drive in O'Henry Oaks

air conditioners to ward off the hot, humid Southern days and nights. We attended all the same schools together: Bessemer Elementary for Grades 1-2; Ceasar Cone Elementary for third and fourth grade; James Y. Joyner Elementary for Grades 5-6; Aycock Junior High (now Melvin C. Swann Jr. Middle School) for seventh and eighth grade; and finally, Walter Hines Page High School.

When we were home, we would often get together with the other kids in the neighborhood to play nerf football in the streets or kick the can on a warm summer evening. Sometimes we'd head down to the playground past Gary's house when we could get enough guys for a game of basketball or tackle football. The football games could get pretty intense because the sidelines were the street or the creek that ran six feet below the playing field. So you either got scraped up or a mouth full of water. David was the better athlete but Gary could hold his own. We were teammates on a Pop Warner football team, the O'Henry Lions, and we played church basketball and softball together through the 16th Street Baptist Church where David's family were members. Gary made it a habit of showing up at

David's house every Sunday evening, never admitting to David until years later that the main reason he did so was because he knew that Mr. Murphy would sometimes order a pizza from Pizza Hut on Sunday nights.

So we knew each other pretty well during those years as kids, but we didn't really become best friends until high school. There's a story about how we wound up at Page High together, and it involves a slice of local history that many people who lived in Greensboro in the late 1970s may recall. From first grade on, our class was the first one in Greensboro public schools that was fully integrated. However, when we were ready to begin high school, the city instituted a plan to further de-segregate the high schools that called for kids in our neighborhood, O'Henry Oaks, to be bused 20 minutes across town to another high school.

Well, Page High was our local school. David's older sisters and Gary's older brother had gone there, and Gary could hear the Page High marching band practice from his front porch. Both of our families wound up working with attorneys to establish other members of our family and friends, who lived in a different neighborhood, as our legal guardians. That's the only way we could manage to attend Page High.

Since Page was not our designated school, we did not have bus service to get there. That meant that David's mom was our "bus" driver. She took us to school almost every morning, and she had a habit of being a bit tardy. It so happened that our school had just tightened its tardy policy to the point where if you arrived late for homeroom three days in a row, you were hit with a one-day suspension. Sure enough, we didn't make it on time for three consecutive days, and while David's homeroom teacher looked the other way, probably because he played football, Gary's homeroom teacher went strictly by the book. With his suspension, Gary not only missed school on the big day of spirit week in the build-up to the big rivalry football game between Page High and Grimsley High, he also had to plow through a list of chores at home as punishment. Ken Allen, a neighborhood friend who would eventually join us at SMO, loves to tell the story about waking up early in the morning to get ready for school and seeing Gary across the street in the driveway, having already begun emptying a truck bed of chopped wood. Gary only reminds David about this about every other day!

Neither of us was what you would call the studious type. I guess you could say we just didn't take school all that seriously—we seldom if ever took a book home and did not keep up with homework assignments. Gary did okay in math but struggled in English and social studies, and he was so lost in Spanish class that he resorted to tucking some study notes in the pull-out drawer of his desk during a test one day. When he got caught, the Spanish teacher directed him to come back at the end of the day and take the test in front of her. Learning a valuable lesson, he would never cheat again. His overall grades were so shaky that he didn't even get an A in gym class!

David had his own academic challenges, not only with Spanish but with chemistry, calculus, English and, well, just about everything except lunch. Looking back, he wonders if he may have had undiagnosed dyslexia. When he received one particularly bad report card during his junior year, he was afraid to show it to his parents. When his father finally got his hands on the list of shaky grades, a little father-son conversation promptly ensued:

"Boy, can you do better than that?"

"Yes, sir."

"Then you better damn well do it!"

Football was David's real focus. He played offensive guard on the Page High football team during a time when it was a state powerhouse under North Carolina Sports Hall of Fame coach Marion Kirby. The Page High Pirates won the state championship while David was on the JV team and finished as state runner-up during his senior year. During his junior year, he informed his coaches that his goal was not just to make it to college ball but to someday play in the NFL.

"Well, I guess you'd better grow about six inches then," he was told. David was just 5-9 and about 215 then. Suffice it to say, he did not grow those six additional inches and climb the ladder to the NFL. In the spring, he played some varsity baseball as a second baseman, soaking up more of the athletic scene at our high school that produced a pro football player, a pro golfer, a pro tennis player, and Danny Manning, a basketball superstar in the class one year behind us who went on to lead Kansas to an NCAA championship and became an NBA All-Star and then an ACC basketball coach at Wake Forest University.

David made several friends among his fellow Page High athletes, and he made sure to make space in that circle for his best buddy Gary. That was a gesture that Gary appreciated more and more as the years rolled by, as some of his own non-athlete friends began turning down the wrong path in life.

We had lots of good times all through those high school years, but it was during those late-night talking sessions on the street corner when our bond really took hold. One night about midnight a police cruiser pulled up to our little meeting spot.

"You boys doing okay?" the officer asked with a stern look.

"Um, yes sir," we answered.

"I see. And do you boys happen to have a flashlight on you?"

"What? No, sir."

"Well, we received a report you all have been walking around shining a flashlight inside some lady's window around the corner."

Although a bit shaken up to be confronted by a Greensboro police-man, we were able to convince that cop that this was a totally false accusa-tion. Turned out that this woman just didn't like us sitting on the street corner near her house. But if she was trying to shut us down, she did not succeed! Perhaps that was an early sign of the perseverance that would later serve us so well.

Sometimes Gary would suggest that we get in the car and cruise High Point Road or check out the scene at the local teen hangouts. But when David would say, "No, I don't think I want to do that," the idea was tabled. We kid each other today that David was already establishing himself as the one that would decide what they would do, while Gary was earning his reputation as the one who would go with the flow.

Since we didn't go out to those teenage hangout joints of Greensboro much, we mostly kept out of trouble. Sometimes we would crank up our music extra loud when we were indoors, especially if the two of us happened to be visiting with Ken. You could say that we had pretty diverse tastes in music, as illustrated by us being among the few kids around who liked the hip hop sounds of Run-DMC and LL Cool J. One night, Gary's mother was driving home when she heard music booming from some nearby house and muttered to herself, "Now what fool is playing music so loud in our neighborhood?" Yep, we were those fools.

Most nights, though, were all about going over to the Fast Fare convenience store just up the street to buy some snacks and play Asteroids on the video game machine—just being best friends during a more innocent time in life. Sometimes we'd sit on the curb at the Fast Fare, chew tobacco and guess what the people entering the store were going to buy. We got pretty good at studying folks because we were right more often than not.

If anyone had tapped us on the shoulder during those long leisurely nights and told us, "You know what, someday you two guys are going to be running a multimillion-dollar janitorial business together," we would have busted our guts laughing. That was NOT what we were seeing for our future in our little crystal balls.

David did have ideas about running his own business someday. In fact, he was going to take over the whole dang business world. His dream image came complete with private jets, multiple homes in exotic places and rising to at least multimillionaire status by age 30. He didn't know exactly what his Fortune 500 business would be, but he never imagined it would be a cleaning business.

The funny thing about that is that David's father ran his own business while David was growing up, and that business just happened to be in... you guessed it, the janitorial business!

When he was very young, David didn't know exactly what his father did for a living. He was just impressed when his dad would sometimes bring home cases of bubble gum, wax lips or ice cream sandwiches. When his father took him to the local discount wholesale store and David saw him talking to a taller man one day, he figured that other person must be

Magnetic sign from Murphy Services days

his father's boss. When he asked about this, he discovered that his dad, Jimmy Murphy, was the boss of his own business: Murphy Services.

This janitorial business began as a side venture while his father held a full-time job as a U. S. Mail Carrier, but it eventually grew large enough to enable Mr. Murphy to give up his postal job and employ as many as 60 workers. Over time, David did his share of janitorial work there. He has fond memories of the days as an 8-year-old when his grandfather, who would help out at Murphy Services from time to time, took him along on cleaning runs to the dental office of Dr. Ditto off Elam Avenue. For his contribution of emptying a few trash cans, David got to take home a prize from the toy chest the doctor kept for his young patients, along with the crisp $1 bill that his grandfather gave him.

A few years later, his dad would sometimes awaken David at about 11 at night and say, "Let's go, boy, time to go to work!" That would happen when one of the Murphy Services' employees had called off working for a late-night job at a grocery store, and David would be pulled in to help strip and refinish the floors. He quickly learned that cleaning was hard work but that when you left that store in the morning with the floors shining like a new penny, you earned a great deal of satisfaction over a job well done. Although there was never a pay check involved, his father would take him out for breakfast on the way home.

Sometimes those overnight strip jobs required a larger crew. On those occasions, David knew just who they should recruit: his best friends Gary and Ken! We both remember the night the three of us joined the crew stripping the floors of a Kroger grocery store half an hour away in Winston-Salem. The routine at that time was that you'd be pretty much locked in the store after closing and be expected to be done by 7 a.m. Working together, we made the time fly. By dawn, we were downright giddy, partly

David, Gary and Ken Allen hanging out in their teens

from having a good time staying up all night and partly, no doubt, from the hours of inhaling that stripper and wax. Ken remembers falling asleep on the way home and Mr. Murphy saying "wake up boy" when we arrived at Susie's Diner in Kernersville, where we all got our fill of tenderloin and gravy biscuits.

The three of us also pitched in together on a Murphy Services construction clean-up job at the site of a new airport Marriott. We would spend hours hauling trash to the dumpster, sweeping up all the dirt and dust from the construction activity and washing down the concrete. David was part of the crew on many other jobs with Murphy Services, while Gary was scrubbing out animals' cages at Dr. White's Americana Animal Hospital, where he had a part-time job, or cutting grass in Irving Park.

For David, most of his janitorial tasks consisted of cleaning office buildings in the evenings after school. However, a drug rehab center that he was assigned to clean could only be done in the afternoon because no one was allowed in the building after hours due to the presence of methadone stored on site.

While cleaning that rehab center with his mother and father, David got a different taste of the life of a janitor. Cleaning buildings at night after they had been closed to the public meant that he was never seen by others, but on this job suddenly lots of people were there to witness him scrubbing toilets and mopping floors. Even though he was performing his cleaning tasks in the company of men and women struggling with addiction or other challenges in life, this was a humbling experience. For the first time, he had come face to face with the stigma of being a janitor, which at that time was probably regarded by most people as being a rung on the ladder below flipping burgers at a burger joint—which some of his friends happened to do. Over time, however, as he learned everything involved with cleaning a building, including stripping and refinishing floors, cleaning carpets and washing windows, being a janitor was something that David learned to embrace and take pride in.

Many years later, we would both dedicate ourselves to helping our own workers rise above the stigma of being a janitor and to feel respected and appreciated for what they did. We'll talk more about that later.

Back then, David had no viable model of how any janitorial business could be successful and sustainable over the long run. Murphy Services, which operated out of a small office next to a barbershop and a convenience store on Phillips Avenue, was not destined to make it over the long haul. David's mother also helped out in the office, and as the years went by David watched his parents fight what seemed like a losing battle in trying to find solid, dependable employees that would work for the low wages that came with the territory. He also would often listen to his mother on the phone with bill collectors, trying to find some arrangement to pay the bills that were overdue. That happened because many of Murphy Services' customers didn't pay their bills on time. Sometimes it was a major hurdle just to make payroll. And then there was the big IRS bill his dad wound up holding after falling behind on paying taxes.

David knew that his father was doing his best. To his dad's credit, he had no college education and no business experience, and he started his business as a part-time job. Yet he was successful in providing a middle-class life for his family while managing to keep the business afloat for many years. But as his father's struggles mounted, David found himself making mental notes on how he would avoid the same kind of pitfalls when he ran his own business someday—the business that he thought would be anything BUT a janitorial company!

As our graduation from Page High School approached, we were both following the same path. On our senior class trip to Myrtle Beach, South Carolina, neither of us could afford a room at the place all our classmates would be staying at on Ocean Drive in North Myrtle Beach, so we just slept in the mobile home that Gary's parents owned at the PirateLand Campground on the south end of Myrtle.

With our shaky grades, it sure didn't seem like we would be college material. However, Gary's cousin, Will Collins, worked at a lab where students from Elon College often completed internships, and he suggested to Gary's dad that Gary should apply to Elon. It so happened at that time that Elon had what seemed like pretty much an open-door policy: if you could pay the tuition and maintain a 2.0 GPA, you could be part of the Elon community. When Gary applied and was accepted during the summer before classes began, David figured, "Hey, if Gary could get in, maybe I can too." And even with his high school GPA of about a 2.3, he made it. We both applied at several of the state universities and Elon was the only school to accept us.

Since living on campus was definitely not in our families' budgets, we had to commute the 30 minutes up Highway 70 to Elon from Greensboro. We rode together when we could, but sometimes our different schedules made that unworkable. Even on those days, we were likely to get together on or around campus for lunch or to just sit in one of our cars catching up between classes.

Back home in Greensboro, we teamed up as assistant coaches for the O'Henry Lions, the same Pop Warner Pee-Wee team we had played on as kids. We can't say it was because of our great coaching, but one season the team made it all the way to a bowl game in Raleigh. Getting there is another one of those stories Gary loves to remind David of today. We drove off for Raleigh in David's Pontiac T-1000, and after riding for an hour or so on I-85 and not seeing any signs for Raleigh exits (in the days long before GPS), we saw a trucking company sign and thought surely they could help us with directions. Gary hadn't really been paying attention to the travel but was sent in to get the directions.

"Get back on the interstate and head toward Greensboro," the man began, and then Gary cut him off.

"But sir, that's not correct," Gary said. "You see, we have been on the road for an hour and we came from Greensboro."

The kind man walked Gary over to a wall map of North Carolina and said, "Well, I don't know about all of that. All I do know is if you want to get to Raleigh, you will need to go through Greensboro." He was moving his finger from "You Are Here" to Greensboro and then to Raleigh as he explained. After a slight pause and with a grimace on his face, Gary said, "Thank you for your help."

Once he set us straight, we realized that we had been heading south, in the wrong direction, and had almost gotten to Charlotte. When we finally arrived in Raleigh, about 2 1/2 hours late, all the other coaches had a pretty good laugh at our little detour. David was the first to admit that he could sometimes become a bit directionally challenged.

We also formed a coaching tandem for the O'Henry Lions Bronco League baseball team for 11 and 12-year-olds. David was the head coach and Gary was his assistant, although he had never really played baseball himself and didn't know all that much about the game. As we soon discovered, we got recruited to coach this team because it was struggling just to get enough players to fill all the positions. Since we didn't have enough kids from our team's assigned neighborhood, we had to take boys that were cut from other teams. In one mismatch, we were on the field so long while the other team batted that we didn't make it beyond the first inning until the allotted game time ran out. We learned some valuable lessons in humility during that season.

College presented us with new academic challenges. Gary, who majored in business finance, was placed on academic warning at Elon at one point. Threatened with the prospect of tumbling into academic probation, he pulled himself up to earn A's and B's. David buckled down enough to earn a 3.6 GPA, and after his sophomore year, a fellow Elon student in the process of transferring to the University of North Carolina in Chapel Hill suggested that David think about applying there as well. Although Chapel Hill was only about an hour from home, David had never set foot on campus and would not have dreamed in a million years that he could ever be accepted there because at the time it was a top 10 school in the country. But he decided to reach higher than he thought he could, and sure enough he was accepted to Carolina. Because he did not have the grades to get into business school, as he had hoped, he settled for a major in political science.

Unfortunately, the academic standards at the major state university were much higher than Elon. As David learned, an academic paper that would have earned him an A at Elon would be graded a C or C-plus at Carolina. He found himself resorting to his old high school study habits, or shall we say his "non-study" habits. He crawled through his first semester with a 1.0 GPA and spent a lot of time over the next couple of years on and off academic warning and probation. David's parents had separated and the financial strain pretty much left him on his own to pay for college, which was now more expensive because he was living on campus. Working just a part-time job to pay expenses often left him scrambling to afford his next meal. David can even remember a few times where he would ask his roommates if he could borrow some bread and bologna for sandwiches until his next paycheck. Meanwhile, Murphy Services had gone out of business, and Mr. Murphy had gone back to work as a U. S. Mail Carrier.

David needed a friend, and once again his old buddy Gary stepped up. Gary had moved into a shared house near Elon, which meant that he was already halfway down the road from Greensboro toward Chapel Hill. Sometimes he'd leave Elon on a Thursday night, skip his Friday classes and stay in David's dorm room until Sunday evening. He even sat in on classes on the UNC campus a few times. We should add that we also became very familiar with the social scene on and off campus. Yes, we had us some good times in Chapel Hill.

Somehow, we both found our way to a college degree. It may have taken Gary 4 ½ years to graduate from Elon, but he wasn't complaining about the extra time since along the way he met his wife Lisa. David continued to wage his ongoing battle with grades, but when he needed to get at least a 3.65 in his final semester to bring his composite GPA up to a 2.0 so he would qualify to graduate in May 1988, in his fifth year of college, he achieved his goal.

So now what? Neither of us had clearly mapped-out goals for the future. While David was at Chapel Hill, he had hoped to pin down some kind of plan for how he would pave his path to entrepreneurial success. But instead, he had struggled just to keep afloat with his grades and graduated saddled with student loans and other debt.

With college degrees in hand, we both ended up back in Greensboro living at home. Gary was promoted to assistant manager at a McDonald's on Randleman Road, where he had first gotten a job with the help of David's sister, Dale, just after high school graduation. He likes to tell the story of when he first started, he was the only white guy on the crew and the others were taking bets on how long he would stay—no one bet on the four-plus years Gary would work there. Although he may not have been raking in a big salary, Gary had used his parents' graduation present to make a down payment on a new 1988 Toyota Celica five-speed and thought he was doing pretty doggone good. Gary's parents had both worked for over 30 years at Sears, Roebuck and Company and from the time he was growing up, Gary always assumed he would go to work for one company and just stay there until retirement like they did.

David was living with his mother and found a part-time, Casual Employee, low-wage job at the post office with the assistance of his father, who had by then worked his way into management. David also became an assistant coach to Marion Kirby on the Page High School football team, assisting with the offensive linemen. Although busy with these commitments, he still had lots of time to think. He had not let go of that idea from childhood that he was going to run his own high-achieving business. But what would that business be, and how would he get started?

David knew that the reality was that he was broke, in debt, and had no money to start his own business and outside of a couple of jobs involving rec programs for the City of Greensboro and brief work handling medical collections for a hospital while in college, he had very little real-world experience. Maybe, he figured, he would just have to start with something he knew. Yes, that was it—he would start his own janitorial business!

CHAPTER 2

Starting Small: $200 and a Borrowed Vacuum Cleaner

The truth is that Gary was not the first person that David reached out to in looking for a partner to start a janitorial service business with him. He tried his mother first.

That seemed like a natural choice. After his parents separated and Murphy Services ended, his mom had begun cleaning houses for a living on her own. She was doing pretty well at it too, and David figured that if they partnered together he could ramp up the residential cleaning side and then expand into commercial cleaning. He gave her lots of good reasons for going into business together, but his mother was having none of it.

"You won't be able to find good people to hire. No one will clean like me," she said, and she added other discouraging predictions. "Your customers won't pay on time, the hours are terrible, and there are a whole bunch of other headaches. Plus, David, you have zero experience running a business."

"Mom, I know you all made a lot of mistakes running Murphy Services, but we can do it differently," David countered. "There are many successful companies around that don't make those same mistakes. There's no reason we can't be successful. Who knows, maybe someday you'll be living on Easy Street."

His mother didn't budge. David could be pretty stubborn himself, but he realized that in this situation the best move was to take his search for a business partner somewhere else...like to his best friend! The talk, as we recall, happened on the front porch of Gary's house on Guest Street.

"It doesn't have to be just a Mom and Pop," David argued. "There are companies out there with thousands of employees doing millions and millions of dollars of business. We can make a real, legit business out of this."

Gary nodded along, but he was actually thinking to himself: *Six months tops. Then, when we see it isn't going to work, we can say, "at least we tried" and get on with our own careers. Anyway, I don't want to deny David the opportunity to pursue his dreams. And we'll get to hang out with each other for awhile, like the old days.*

"Sure, count me in," Gary finally said out loud.

Our business partnership had begun.

We leaped into action, with each of us putting in a whopping $100 in start-up funds to open a bank account. Gary likes to tell the story that David was so broke, he had to borrow the $100 from his Visa card to kick in his share. To be equals, we decided to call our business MC Cleaning Service, using the first initials of our last names for the "MC" part. We created a business card with each of our names on it and a simple tagline: "We'll do good by you."

We went "all-out" for supplies to launch our operation. Gary's mother let us borrow her old Sears Kenmore canister vacuum cleaner, and we scrounged around the shed in back of David's Mom's house to come up

MC Cleaning Service business card

MC Cleaning Service

"We'll do good by you."
- Commercial • Industrial cleaning
- New construction cleaning
- Floor maintenance

David Murphy
Gary Collins   Phone: 621-2580

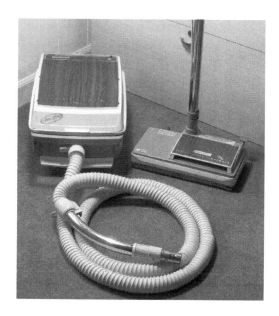

The Sears Kenmore vacuum borrowed from Gary's mother

with a couple of rusted out metal mop buckets, a few large trash buggies and a 1970's NSS electric floor burnisher from the Murphy Services days. Gary's parents chipped in the use of a computer and dot matrix printer they kept in their spare bedroom. We carefully weighed all the "major" early decisions: do we buy 50 envelopes or 100? Gary thought 50 should be enough for six months, but David insisted on buying 100, which was the better value. With only $200 we had to stretch it a long way.

We knew we needed some kind of office as the base of our operations. Since David's mother lived in a three-bedroom house and she slept in one room and David in another, that left one bedroom vacant. Although she thought the whole idea was crazy, David's mom gave us the go-ahead to call that spare room our office.

Now all we needed were some customers. We got our business phone line set up and took out a very small ad in the Yellow Pages, which we thought was very expensive. We waited and waited and...nothing.

By the first of the year, 1989, David came up with the idea that MC Cleaning Service sounded too much like a Mom and Pop. We needed to change our name to something more professional, a catchy phrase more aligned with David's image of becoming an international conglomerate. So we sat down and brainstormed possibilities, finally winnowing it down to a choice between the words "superior" and "supreme." In the end, "supreme" won out. We also figured we should take the word "cleaning" out of the title because, after all, we were going to be much more than that. That's how Supreme Maintenance Organization, or SMO, as it has become known as, was born in January 1989.

Finally, we landed our first job: cleaning up a rental property after one tenant moved out and the next one was about to move in. Determined to make an excellent first impression, we cleaned that place top to bottom. It took us an entire week, but when we were done everything was spotless and sparkling. The only problem was that the old, brittle windows with the wood frame and the caulking were not quite up to the challenge of our gung-ho cleaning approach. Yep, we broke two windows on our first job. We had charged the customer $216 for the job, but after paying for the broken windows, it didn't leave us any profit. We were not discouraged, though. We got our feet wet, and the sky was the limit!

To keep rolling, we were willing to take any paying job we could find. We hauled trash, did some landscaping work and actively solicited clean-up jobs at new home construction sites. With a little persistence, we began to develop a little niche cleaning up high-end, newly constructed homes. We vividly recall that time early on when we accepted the assignment to clean three large homes, one with 12,000 square feet, so they would be ready to be shown in the local Showcase of Homes. It was a last-minute clean-up because home construction projects always run late, and the cleaners were supposed to be the last one in, but we were up for the challenge. It just meant that we pretty much didn't sleep for 36 hours straight.

At that time, we were both still working our part-time day jobs from 5 to 10 a.m., Gary at McDonald's, where he was so good at what he did that he once won a drive-thru All-American contest, and David at the post office. As soon as we got off work at 10 a.m., we would rush to the new homesite and work all day and through the night, only stopping at

4:30 a.m. to get ourselves cleaned up and presentable for our day jobs starting at 5 a.m. At 10 a.m., we'd head right back to the construction clean-up. That routine marked the first of many long days and double-days.

We began obtaining some significant leads from people that we knew. David's dad led us toward a contract to clean a few post office branches. Fred Joseph, one of the assistant football coaches at Page High, offered additional customer prospects while also putting us in contact with accountants and insurance specialists who guided us in setting up our business the right way. Mr. J., as we affectionately called him, also helped us establish a banking relationship and later was critical in helping us secure our first bank loan.

During this time, we had several friends who came to work with us as we struggled to get it all done. Anthony "Roni" Oliver, who was an old high school football teammate of David's and coached with him at Page, was always there to help us clean the post offices or strip and wax their floors on an all-night shift. Addison Edwards, a friend we got to know who also coached football with us, also helped us clean post offices and some of

Our first publicity photo, circa 1989

our other jobs. Babette Weaver Smith, a family friend, also helped us out on many cleaning jobs and John Newman, who wrote the Foreword for this book, even helped us out from time to time. While many friends were doubting us, it was great to have friends that we knew we could count on and trust to help us out during those early days.

In June of that first year, we secured a substantial contract job cleaning part of a 12-story condominium tower. Every morning, we cleaned the first-floor banquet rooms, offices and other common areas. When we obtained a few other contract cleaning accounts, we were able to let go of the construction clean-ups and even give up our day jobs. We finished our first year with a whopping revenue total of $23,393.82. It wasn't much but it was a start.

We need to point out that even getting that far would not have been possible without the generous support of Gary's father, Paul Collins. He let us borrow his rusted out, puke green 1971 Chevy C10 pickup truck to complete some of those early jobs. We added some homemade wooden fence sidewalls so we could increase the payload of trash that we hauled. We often joked that we probably looked like Sanford and Son in that old truck and even hummed the theme song from that TV show while driving around town.

Early on during that first year operating SMO, Mr. Collins also provided us a critical loan of $3,000. He made sure that we took this very seriously, issuing a handwritten promissory note that stipulated that we would begin monthly payments one month after issuance of the loan and that "negligence to pay may result in a late fee of $5 per week."

We were extremely grateful for his assistance at our time of need. Since there was a local bank at the time named First Home Federal, we would respectfully joke that we had borrowed money from "First Home Paul." We paid back that loan and we've held onto that promissory note all these years as a reminder of where we came from and the help we received along the way. When we recently mentioned that old loan to Gary's father, he asked us if the promissory note had ever been marked as paid in full. When we noticed that it had not been so noted, Gary

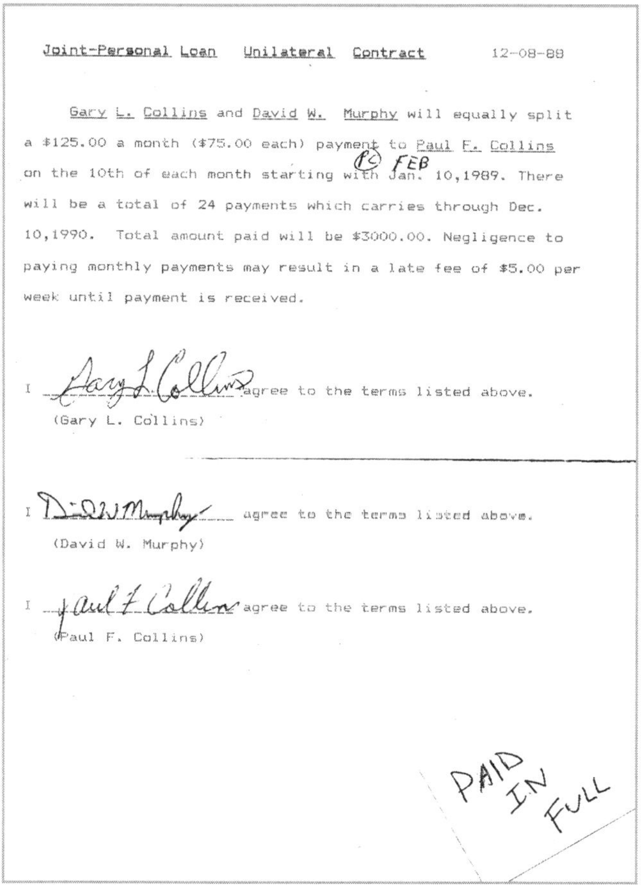

```
Joint-Personal Loan   Unilateral  Contract      12-08-88


    Gary L. Collins and David W.  Murphy will equally split
a $125.00 a month ($75.00 each) payment to Paul F. Collins
on the 10th of each month starting with Jan. 10,1989. There
will be a total of 24 payments which carries through Dec.
10,1990.  Total amount paid will be $3000.00. Negligence to
paying monthly payments may result in a late fee of $5.00 per
week until payment is received.



I  _____ agree to the terms listed above.
   (Gary L. Collins)



I  _____ agree to the terms listed above.
   (David W. Murphy)


I  _____ agree to the terms listed above.
   (Paul F. Collins)
```

(handwritten: *CS FEB*)

(handwritten: *PAID IN FULL*)

Our promissory note to Paul Collins

immediately wrote "Paid in Full" across the front.

We don't remember this for sure, but we're fairly certain that we found ourselves going back to "First Home Paul" when we ran into a little problem some months after hiring our first employees. With David's father's history of owing a bunch of money to the IRS, we were smart enough to begin taking out payroll taxes from the beginning and were very careful to refer to the right chart and deduct the proper amount from each employee's check. What we weren't smart enough to understand was that you are supposed to send those withholdings to the IRS on a regular schedule. Oops! We learned of this mistake through some "friendly" correspondence from the IRS, informing us that we owed several thousand dollars in unpaid taxes and penalties. We weathered that little storm thanks to "First Home Paul" and, needless to say, never missed another payroll tax deposit.

Interviewing our first job candidates outside of our family and friends was a bit awkward. Because we still hadn't gotten a "real" office, we had to meet with our prospective employees in David's mother's living room. After mumbling an apology, we told the truth: "Look, this is who we are. We're just getting started. But we're not a scam—you'll get paid for your work."

That seemed to convince the interviewees, and by the second year our little company was beginning to grow. We added new accounts, especially the post offices, and finished 1990 with $61,023.45 in revenue. That may not sound like much, but the way we looked at it, we had nearly tripled our revenue in one year.

Of course, even after quitting our outside jobs we were pretty doggone tired most of the time. On a typical day, we might start with cleaning a post office building from 8 in the morning until 2 in the afternoon, then huddle in our "office" for a few hours to attend to business upkeep tasks before going back out around 5:30 p.m. for our "second shift," which meant cleaning until 1 or 2 a.m. As young and full of energy as we were, we still had to catch little ways to get some rest. There were many a day while we were cleaning those condominium towers that we would plop down in a hidden corner of the banquet room for a moment's respite that somehow turned into 30 minutes or an hour.

Our late-night routines would sometimes find us briefly laying on the floor of a lobby of some building we had finished cleaning and just talking, laughing and relaxing for a few minutes. Next thing we knew, we'd look at the clock, see that it was 3 a.m., and say, "Uh-oh, we've got to get out of here!"

If anybody had kept a tape recorder to capture what we would talk about during those post-midnight breaks, they'd probably hear us making fun of ourselves constantly: "Here we are, two college graduates out cleaning toilets at two o'clock in the morning. What the heck are we doing?" Naturally, we would talk about our cleaning business sometimes, but we also had a chance to share more about our personal lives, including the many sacrifices made by David's wife Paula and Gary's wife Lisa, who both somehow put up with our impossibly long hours. It was no joke that at David's home, "date night" for a couple of years consisted of Paula accompanying David on a late-night cleaning run. At Gary's house, Lisa slowly came to accept that just because Gary wanted to get home for dinner, the reality was that on many nights, "dinner" would have to wait until 8 or 10…or maybe midnight. At one point, Lisa and Paula banded together in support of our families' income by operating a laundry service for dentists and hygienists.

Talking about our lives late at night on those cleaning sites was a bit like being back on the street corner near our homes as teenagers, when we would just sit under that street light and talk and talk. Of course, there was one major difference: when we got done talking now, we still had work to do before we could go home and get to bed. As Gary remembers it, David would sometimes head off on a fast-food run to keep us replenished during these late-night operations, and sometimes he would be gone an awfully long time while Gary had to go right on working. David insists that he has no memory of any such occasions!

We're more in sync with the memory of something else we did to keep our spirits afloat during those long nights of cleaning, which usually came on the heels of the long DAYS of cleaning. When we were kidding around about our crazy schedules one time, we started thinking up a little song about who we were and what we did. After more than 25 years, we can still recall the lyrics:

We are the men from SMO
And we can give you mo'
We give you mo'
And nothing less
We are the best
We are the best!

You had to be there to fully appreciate the creativity and splendor of our songwriting skills and the smooth voices (well, for one of us anyway!) that would belt out the words in perfect harmony at one o'clock in the morning. We were always on the lookout for any little thing we could do to maintain our sanity.

Our third year, 1991, ushered in a major change: we finally moved out of the spare room in David's mother's house and set up in our own "real" office! It wasn't much, really, just two small rooms in a little office next to a barbershop in the Mill Village on 4th Street. Since we couldn't afford to make a professional sign to hang outside the entrance, we asked a friend to trace our logo on a chunk of wood. We probably paid him a few bucks for the materials. We used one of the two rooms for storage and crammed our desks in across from each other a few feet apart in the other room. Our revenue, however, did not register a major change, only inching up to $72,682.73. We would try to laugh that off, declaring that we were "on our way to $.1 million." But friends and family watching how we were working so hard for so little money had a different perspec-

Our first office on 4th Street

tive—they thought we had absolutely lost our minds!

Gary's father-in-law Bob Haug had an estate attorney friend from the bank in which he worked for in Northern Virginia, and he thought it would be a good idea to have her evaluate our business since evaluating companies was her specialty. After submitting our financials, we patiently waited for the results. Bob had hoped that she would have some positive results and encouraging news, but when the letter came back stating we should dissolve our business as soon as possible because it was not sustainable with two owners, Bob decided he wasn't going to share the letter. Not until Gary asked Bob repeatedly for the results did Bob reluctantly share the professional advice. At first, Gary thought, well the letter says we will not be successful so I guess we will need to shut the doors. David, however, had a different thought: ignore it! We don't know if we were too dumb or just too stubborn to heed this expert advice, but we went right on doing what we were doing—using another doubting opinion for motivation and trying to earn a living with our little cleaning business. That business advisor might have known our financials, but she didn't know us or our determination. While Bob hasn't offered any additional free evaluations, he has continued to be an excellent encourager to Gary and his family.

At least we were smart enough to realize that we had to make some adjustments. At some point, David turned to Gary and offered him "The Deal" as it became known: "If you get me out of day to day cleaning so I can focus on growing the business, in six months I'll get you out of the day to day cleaning too." Gary was a little apprehensive about accepting David's offer because the agreement had always been that they would share the workload 50-50 and he figured he would get the short end of the stick. Gary knew he was tired of cleaning all the time and didn't have much to lose so he decided to accept "The Deal" and prayed David could hold up his end of the bargain.

We figured it out, though, and made the change to enable David to focus on growing the business. Luckily, things worked out and we were both able to relinquish our daily cleaning responsibilities. However, we still had to get over some other bumps together as we sorted out who we were and what each of us would do in our working partnership. It was great to have that foundation of being best friends, but the other side of the picture was that we had to learn how to get along in running a business together. We were still just a couple of young, immature kids really. In the beginning, we don't think we even gave ourselves titles, although David remembers putting down "General Manager" for David and "Operations Manager" for Gary to complete some insurance forms. As we took our time sorting through many other questions about our responsibilities, our roles slowly began to take shape.

Since Gary had a degree in finance from Elon, he started out as the bookkeeper. But after an error or two, it was decided that David would take over that role. When it came time to make a proposal to a potential customer, however, we would present ourselves together as a team. We even dressed up in suits and ties to convince our prospects that we were a *very* professional business. There was one particular time that we had gotten an opportunity to bid on a building where one of David's family members worked and we wanted to make a great impression with our proposal. We realized that our little three-page proposal was due for an upgrade, which by the way, we are continuously upgrading even today. So we literally stayed up all night working on that proposal, reminding us of a college all-nighter. (As a matter of fact, our sales team will sometimes pull an all-nighter even today to meet a large bid proposal due date. They have even joked about getting matching SMO pajamas!) Anyway, we added a lot of details about our little company, including color graphics and charts, and we added a real contract. We were so proud. We won the bid but David's family member pointed out one small error. On the top of our introduction letterhead it read that we were "Boned and Insured." It should have read "Bonded and Insured." We were so embarrassed, although we joked about it for a long time.

We also did most of the hiring together, figuring that when it came to deciding who would and would not be a good fit to join our humble company, two heads were better than one. For almost any big decision impacting the business, the two of us would discuss it and chart our course to follow as a team.

The business was making inroads here and there until one day our first big break arrived. We wish we could say that it came about directly from our dedicated efforts at making cold calls, tracking leads and showing potential customers just what SMO could do for them. But we have to admit that this breakthrough account just showed up at our doorstep—well, actually the phone's handset. We got the job because our phone number in that Yellow Pages ad happened to begin with the same three-digit prefix as this future customer's phone number. They figured that if we were in the same Greensboro neighborhood, they could probably trust us.

It was September 1992 when we got that call from the new Kmart Distribution Center (DC). Their initial offer didn't knock our socks off, just buffing their cafeteria floors once a week. But once we got out there, we were able to land a contract to provide daily cleaning services for all their front office space, along with their break rooms and restrooms, five days a week. That was a nice, solid account, bringing in about $4,000 per month. And, just as we did with all our customers, we treated Kmart DC and the work we did for them as the most important part of our operation. We knew from our first days with SMO that if we were going to grow and succeed, we had to regard every customer as if they were the biggest one because someday they might be.

Which is exactly what happened with the Kmart DC. Two years after we got our mops in the door, the distribution center was going through some changes with their labor. They came to us with a question: would we be willing to take a little test to see if we might be suitable for an expanded cleaning role, which might involve cleaning the whole facility on the third shift? Of course we were going to say yes to a question like that, but we soon found out that this was not going to be an easy hoop to jump through. The test was to detail clean all the restroom complexes from top to bottom in the distribution center's 1.6 million square foot facility...with just the weekend to get it done!

There was no way that we were going to back down from the challenge, so we pulled out all the stops to rise up to meet it. We were soon calling everyone in both our families, as well as all our friends, our fellow church members, and anyone else we could think of to ask (or beg!) to come help us out. We put together a sizeable army of cleaners, most with no professional cleaning experience and no interest in ever obtaining a regular janitorial position. We had teachers, we had nurses, we had just about every other profession represented. And, with a couple of 16-hour days, darn if we didn't pull it off!

When Monday morning dawned, our army of 20-plus paid volunteers had passed that test with all A's, something we had never known all those years in school. Mike Davidson, the Facility Manager, was so impressed that he offered us the opportunity to take over the third shift housekeeping operation for the entire distribution center. Not long after that, they added the second shift, and then later the first shift to our responsibilities. Eventually, this expansion grew into an account that yielded just over $1 million in revenue per year, with 55 full-time employees working three shifts to make it all happen. SMO was on the map and would become a serious player in the local janitorial service industry!

We can't remember everything we did to appropriately thank our army of helpers that made this breakthrough possible, but whatever we did, it was not enough. Because all those men and women believed in us and were willing to roll up their sleeves to meet the challenge presented to us, we were able to make one giant stride in our growth at a time when we badly needed a push in the right direction. So, one more time, we want to take this opportunity to say THANK YOU, THANK YOU, THANK YOU!!!

Of course, having one big break did not mean we suddenly had it all figured out and knew everything we needed to know to successfully maintain and continue to build a larger company. The truth is, we had a lot to learn about practically everything, and we were fortunate to have many people to help open our eyes and ears.

One major eye-opener was attending our first BSCAI (Building Service Contractors Association International) convention. In 1993, the annual convention was held in Atlanta, which meant we could easily drive down and save money on airfare. As two best friends just trying to get a simple cleaning business to take root in Greensboro, we were overwhelmed to find ourselves surrounded by hundreds of vendors and cleaning business owners, some of whom were leading operations with hundreds or even thousands of employees working in several states. We attended almost all of the peer-to-peer classes, each offering at least one piece of new information that we could put to immediate or long-term use. As we soon discovered, though, the real learning happened when you just sat down on a sofa and started talking to some other business owner. We were amazed at how willing most of them were to openly share their experiences and ideas with a couple of new guys on the block. We can remember meeting Greg Littlefield, Past President of the BSCAI, and his colleagues with PFMI, a Building Service Contractor based in Montgomery, Alabama. It felt like we had known them for years as we shared stories and ideas, and we still maintain that relationship today.

David soon learned that he could make other helpful contacts by volunteering to serve on a BSCAI committee. At first he felt a bit intimidated, but the veteran members took him in and treated him as an equal. One colleague, Ron Goerne, who was a past BSCAI President, invited David to come to Bloomington, Illinois to gain a close-up look at his own successful cleaning company. During his on-site visit, David was invited to offer his input into a training program Ron's team was developing at the time. He soaked up everything he could, including a key lesson about staffing. Although Ron's business had grown to several million dollars in revenue, he maintained only a small administrative staff. Working in a thin-margin industry, it was always going to be necessary to keep a lean administrative staff.

David also came away from that visit, and other discussions with fellow owners of cleaning companies, with a reassurance that SMO was on the right track on one important front. By then we had already established a clear chain of command among our employees, so that everyone knew who reported to whom and who answered to whom. In our line of work, especially, organization and a solid sense of structure were critical.

David had witnessed the importance of organization and structure while working with Coach Marion Kirby and his staff on the Page High football team. During those first few years of revving up his role as co-founder of SMO, David continued to serve as an assistant coach at Page. It didn't take him long to understand that being part of those high-achieving Pirates' teams was teaching him valuable lessons that could be put to good use in his own business.

Frank Starling, long-time Page offensive line coach, emphasized the phrase "Proper Preparation Prevents Poor Performance." All of Page's practices were meticulously planned down to the last minute, with each coach required to keep the schedule in his back pocket. Every Sunday during football season all the coaches would get together and spend hours and hours studying game film, breaking down their next opponent and developing a game plan for that week's game. Everything Coach Kirby did was extremely well organized and highly structured. That's what David brought over to his role in running SMO.

Gary's early management style was formed from the managers that he observed while working at McDonald's. Whether it was Buddy Haithcock's (who just happens to be David's cousin) ability to be the top dog AND teach "If it's fun, it gets done", or Ron Surgeon promoting "High Energy... High Energy!", Veronica Jones showing Gary her trust and confidence she had with him, or Russell Burris taking care of business while remaining one of the boys, Gary noticed and absorbed it all. While Gary received an education from Elon, it was in the grill area, front counter and servicing the general public at McDonald's where Gary learned to deal with people.

So we were doing some things right, and we had scored that first big break. We no longer had to interview potential employees in David's mom's living room, and we were providing jobs for dozens of employees. But we'd be lying if we said that everything was humming like a well-oiled machine.

We made mistakes that reminded us that we didn't know what we didn't know. We still lived with major day-to-day uncertainty about what new fires would need to be put out, or whether the plug might be pulled on any of our accounts, big or small. And the two of us continued to work 70- or 80-hour weeks. Although our revenues had increased, we were still limited by the thin profit-margin in this industry that we had chosen. We had yet to see any truth to the reassurances that we would sometimes hear that sounded something like, "Oh, you're in the janitorial business? There's a lot of money in the janitorial business!" It took us a long time to realize that people making such confident pronouncements were really just trying to make us feel better about being "only" janitors. There was still that stigma floating around.

Not in our minds, though. We were proud of what we were doing and tried to extend that sense of pride to everyone who worked for us. But with all the challenges we battled every day, we couldn't help getting frustrated sometimes. Actually, it was probably more like MANY times that one or the other of us might say or think something about quitting. We leaned on one another during those moments, as we always did. One time it might be David who was tempted to give it all up, and Gary would help him to hang in there, and the next time it would be Gary considering the idea of quitting and David would help talk him out of it.

Once, Gary received a message from another source that was so powerful, and that went in so deep, that he remembers almost every word of it today. Here's the story, and it's a good thing Gary's not telling it to you in person because if he did, you would probably see him start to choke up before he'd get past the opening scene.

Gary was out in the parking lot of our 4th Street office on that warm summer evening, during one of those typical late-night moments of frustration. David didn't happen to be around, but John Headen, one of our most dedicated employees at the time, was there to lend an ear. John had only been with us a year or so, but there was something about him that just made you trust him. Gary also knew that John, like Gary, was a Christian, so he allowed himself to spill out some of those frustrations about working days and nights, 14 to 16 hours a day and how he just wasn't sure how much longer he could continue the madness. Gary knew that John worked

John Headen

full time at North Carolina A&T State University and worked at SMO part time, but he was not as familiar with another part of John's background.

"Let me tell you something," John began, looking Gary right in the eyes in the dim street light. "I used to run a courier biz, but I got out of it. Yes, I quit. Looking back, you know why I quit? It was Satan telling me to do it. I should never have listened to him, but I did."

Now that he had Gary's full attention, John went on:

"Gary, I don't want to see you make the same mistake that I made. So every time you feel like you want to quit, just remind yourself that's Satan telling you that. He knows how God can use you and your company for the Glory of God. Do not ever give in to Satan's desires. Keep pressing on."

After that night, something changed for Gary. Before his talk with John, every time he felt like quitting it would drain his energy and desire. Even though he still occasionally felt that urge to give it up, he would remember John's words and feel a sense of renewed energy, and the reassurance that by sticking with his role in co-steering Supreme Maintenance Organization, he was doing the right thing; he was helping to do God's work, and you never regret making the right decision.

As it turned out, John didn't stay with us all that long. But he had been the right person at the right time with the right message. On that warm summer night, John had spoken to Gary like an angel.

CHAPTER 3

Perseverance:
The Bedrock of Our Success

People sometimes ask us to name our proudest accomplishment in building a cleaning business that has lasted 30 years and counting, and how we've grown into a multimillion-dollar operation that serves an expanding regional market. There are many ways we can explain it, but it can probably all be boiled down to one simple word: perseverance.

One way or another, we've made it through all the changes and challenges, the wins and losses, the downturns in the economy and the mistakes of our own making. Perseverance is what carried us through what we call the "manure years" when we trudged our way through those ridiculously long hours and couldn't see the light at the end of the tunnel. And perseverance and grit have swept us along through all those times when we would dare to take our next step without knowing where our feet would land. Despite many pitfalls, we somehow just kept going. Perseverance produced character, and character produced hope, and it was our perseverance that gave us an endless hope.

We definitely had to tap that spirit of perseverance when we faced our first major loss. In 1998, the Kmart distribution center that was still our bread and butter experienced some internal changes. They had turned over their general manager and facilities manager, which meant that the relationships we had invested so much in with the previous people in those positions were suddenly worthless. We had been around long enough by then to understand that most new facility managers in our business were apt to rely on their own established relationships in building a team around them. They would also be looking to make an immediate impact, and if that meant saving the company a few bucks on cleaning services in the short-term, that's probably what they were going to do.

Sure enough, Kmart DC suddenly decided to go in a different direction with its cleaning operations. Just like that, 50 percent of our business was gone and 55 full-time SMO employees suddenly had no place to work! We knew that having the plug pulled on our operation had nothing to do with any failure on our part to provide a quality service, but that didn't matter. However, we didn't do a good job of treating the new facility management team like they were a new customer. We thought we could rest on our laurels. And now we were cast adrift and had to figure out if there was any way to keep our boat from sinking.

To be honest, our initial thought was "That's it, we're done. We made a good run at it, it was fun while it lasted, but it's time to man the lifeboats." One life lesson we had already learned was, when perseverance becomes your habit, quitting is not an option. No, bailing out was not our way. We had taken to heart those messages from the voice of God through John Headen and many other sources that leading SMO was providing us with an opportunity to serve. We had to remind ourselves that God always knows what's best for us. Maybe this Kmart DC door was closing because another door was waiting to be opened? After all, sometimes good things fall apart so better things can fall together.

We didn't immediately know quite how that was going to work, but we did know one thing. While some business experts will tell you that when you lose half your business you've got to start cutting staff, we were not going to leave behind our most important asset: our key people. We soon set up private talks with Al Summers, who had taken over the role of Account Manager with the Kmart DC, and Diana Wilson, a promising and dedicated Sales Representative. We invited them individually to meetings with the two of us at a McDonald's on West Market Street, just up the street from our office. Because we had not yet announced the loss of the Kmart DC account to our staff, we wanted to get outside the office to avoid any unnecessary whispering of bad news filtering through the ranks.

"At first I wondered why we weren't having the meeting in the office," Diana recalls. "Then when we sat down together at McDonald's, David and Gary showed me the cancellation letter explaining that we had lost the Kmart DC account. I knew there had been recent issues, but it was still a major setback. Then they said, 'We don't know exactly what our future holds, but no matter who we lose business with, we want you to know that we are committed to keeping you on board. Your job is secure with us.' I took them at their word. I knew that I could trust them."

That's the only way we knew how to handle the challenge that had been dropped on our laps. These two loyal employees had done nothing wrong, so why should we abandon these leaders? They had been giving the company more than 100 percent, often at great personal sacrifice. And if this setback proved to be temporary, as we hoped, we were going to need them. We were going to persevere together and keep seeing what was around the bend.

And then that new door really did open. The seeds for this next big break had been planted shortly before we lost the Kmart DC. Gary's friend Ron F. approached him at church and asked if we would be willing to clean the High Point site of a major logistics company. We agreed right away, and even though the account was just for one person working five hours a day, we welcomed this new business, remembering the importance of treating every customer as if they are the biggest and most important one because someday they may be.

Sure enough, not long after the Kmart DC loss had hit us, we won a bid with that logistics company to clean their main location in Greensboro. This added business was going to employ a crew of 12 to 15 cleaners and generate another $350,000 in annual revenue. The new project was slated to begin April 1st, 1998, and Gary was so excited that he figured he would get a laugh from his buddy Ron by playing a little April Fool's Day joke on him. He knew that Ron would be showing up around 7 that morning, and although our team had already been on the job two hours by then, Gary was going to intercept Ron before he could see the results of our labor and tell him something like, "Ron, I'm really sorry—our people didn't show up." Fortunately, Gary decided to stick his plan for that April Fool's Day prank back in his pocket. Sometimes it's just not a good idea to mix friendship with business and while Gary felt good about his personal relationship with Ron, he wanted to keep it strictly professional at work.

We were grateful for this opportunity and tried to show it by how well we cleaned that facility. And it really needed cleaning! From the looks of things, that place had not been cleaned by the previous cleaning contractor in weeks. We had all hands on deck. David, Gary, Al and Diana were all on site to ensure that we got off to a good start. We just worked and worked, staying much later than we anticipated, and enjoyed that sense of accomplishment that comes when you thoroughly clean something that had been really, really dirty. The real surprise came the next morning. When we arrived for our second day of cleaning this new account, we found the facility just as dirty as it had been the first day. We figured out that in that kind of operation, things just got dirty really fast every day.

We continued to do our best, trying to convince this company that we could be trusted and that we could successfully take on added responsibilities. Over time, we added their facility in Charlotte and a few others outside of Charlotte, and we extended into Raleigh as well. At one point, we were servicing a total of 17 sites for this company.

We're going to do a quick fast-forward on our history with this customer to illustrate another way that perseverance has become vital to our growth and success. Around 2008, at a time when this account was already generating a substantial portion of our business, the client decided to regionalize their bid rather than accepting bids for individual facilities. We put in an aggressive bid for North Carolina, South Carolina, Virginia, Georgia and a couple of other states. When they came back to us, they told us they were interested in having us take over North and South Carolina, and Virginia as well, if we were willing to revisit our proposal. We adjusted accordingly and suddenly had reached an agreement to go from cleaning 17 sites to almost 100 sites in three states.

That kind of internal customer growth reminded us of how we had started small with the Kmart DC before expanding into a substantially larger account. To see it happening again was certainly exciting, but this new opportunity brought with it many new challenges. We were used to meeting the needs of increased staff, and as we will talk about in the next chapter, our people have always delivered for us and made it possible for us to grow and thrive. Even the need to hire 100-plus people did not faze us. However, it takes more than hiring dozens of new employees to step up and meet this kind of expansion. When we crunched the numbers regarding the financial impact of our new regional business, we figured that we would have to go out and buy half-a-million dollars' worth of equipment to handle that much cleaning at so many different locations.

Well, that kind of investment was enough to lead Ken, our Corporate Controller, to question whether we should really take all this on. We were determined to go forward, however, and we met the new hiring challenge with a three-month, all-hands-on-deck commitment that required us to interview and hire additional employees at about 80 new cleaning sites. David even enlisted his 15-year-old daughter to hit the road with him to help manage the sea of job candidates to be interviewed.

Pulling together the needed personnel was happening in a timely enough way, but scrounging up the funds required for such a large project was proving to be a bit more difficult. We approached our regular bankers, people with whom we had built solid relationships, and told the truth right up front: "Hey guys, we've got this bid and we're going to need some help with equipment. We're looking at half a million dollars."

At first, we were assured that the loan would not be a problem. Unfortunately, the timing, in late '08 and early '09, soon meant that "Houston, we have a problem." As most of us remember, the banking world was being turned upside down on its head at that time. "Guys, I'm afraid we can't do this for you after all," our bankers informed us. Undaunted, we turned to a community bank where we had done some business in the past and made our pitch to them. Fortunately, they came through with that big loan. If that bank had not stepped up, we're not sure what we would have done, except that we still would not have given up. We would persevere no matter what. But with everything falling into place for this major expansion, we could bow our heads and acknowledge that, once again, God had provided for us.

Soon we were buying so much equipment that we could barely manage the flow in and out of our office in Greensboro. It was a new task for us to start marking cleaning supplies and equipment by writing, "This is for Virginia," "This is for South Carolina," "This is for North Carolina." We figured it out, though, and just kept going forward, and we're still cleaning the entire region for that logistics company today.

Just as our Kmart DC account had put us on the map as a cleaning business, this new business expanded that map. In more recent years, our expansion also has taken us into cleaning schools. Again, we started small, cleaning only a few private and charter schools. Then we got a break by securing the contract to clean at a large community college, and by treating each of those schools as our most important customer we put ourselves in position to be considered for other school contracts. We're up to 35 schools and colleges as we write this, so this is another example of how our growth is often internal, with one customer or within one industry. Every time we expand, we do whatever it takes to make it happen even if it feels like we are flying by the seat of our pants. That's our spirit of perseverance in action.

Perseverance also shows up in how we deal with customer complaints, or "opportunities" as we like to call them. Now, we need to point out first that the cleaning business is a great industry and we have been overwhelmingly blessed with many wonderful and loyal customers. Several of them have stuck with us for many, many years, and often treat us and our people as if we are a part of their business or organization. Many customers have become our friends. However, even the best customers sometimes have opportunities that we need to address.

Right from the early days, we had to get used to receiving calls from customers who would sometimes report a minor problem, like the one trash can our people missed in their building. Whenever this happens, even today, we always apologize and strive to do better. But the reality is that cleaners are going to miss a trash can or make some other kind of oversight now and then. People are human, and no matter how hard they try or how dedicated they are, they're going to mess up once in a while. (Robots are not ready just yet to take over all cleaning tasks.) We understand that, and we treat our employees with as much empathy and compassion as we can. Unfortunately, customers don't always understand the reality about the inevitable mistakes that will happen from time to time in the cleaning process. They sometimes think, "This is so simple, how can they mess it up?"

It is always nice to work with customers who have our back and understand that as humans we are sometimes going to make mistakes. We remember that time when a customer in a medical facility received a complaint from one of the nurses about one missed trash can. The customer responded with this reality check for the nurse: "Let's put this in perspective. If we have 500 trash cans and they miss one, that's a 99.8 percent efficiency rate. Tell me something, do you think our own employees operate at a 99.8 percent level of efficiency?" He went on to say, "Now go empty your trash can into a bigger one. If they miss another one, then let me know."

As Vice President of Operations, Gary is in communication with the frontlines every day and personally deals with customer opportunities to improve customer relations and build trust. He says that like a boxer in the ring, every opportunity is like a body blow (some are bigger than others) and it is hard not to sometimes take these issues personally. When Gary occasionally moans about feeling exhausted from those body blows, David listens compassionately. Then he adds, "If this was easy, anybody could do it." Then Gary feels better and gets back up and starts correcting those issues and rebuilding the customers' trust. In other words, we have that extra layer of perseverance that helps us take on whatever challenges come our way.

Sometimes what comes as a specific complaint from a customer is not even our company's fault. If something turns up missing or stolen from a building where a cleaner works at night, guess who's going to be presumed guilty the minute the discovery is made the next morning? You bet, it's the cleaner.

We once had a situation where a customer accused one of our employees of stealing a pair of prescription sunglasses. Now, what are the chances that this employee would just happen to have the exact same prescription as the customer's employee who reported the missing glasses? Feeling pretty confident that our employee didn't take the glasses, we still paid to replace them. It's just necessary sometimes to maintain good customer relations. That accusation was eventually dropped for a very good reason: the person found the glasses in some unexpected place where they had left them.

In a case of a more serious accusation, one customer from a large company that we cleaned called Gary one day and informed him that our night-time cleaner had been going into the executive's office, opening up the safe and stealing money out of it. Now, this was no Fisher-Price toy safe we're talking about; it was a very sturdy and sophisticated safe that our cleaner, supposedly, had somehow figured out how to crack. The customer even offered as "proof" a shadow on the wall captured by video surveillance during the time our cleaner was in the building.

We were certainly not presuming guilt on the part of our employee, but we had to take the accusation seriously enough to offer the customer our surveillance equipment, which was concealed in a boom box, to see what may have been going on involving our cleaner. Weeks went by, and not a word from our customer. Finally, after about two months, Gary called to follow up. "Oh, you can come pick up your equipment now," he was told, with no further explanation. We tracked down the explanation ourselves. One of our managers had built a close relationship with a security guard at that building, and the guard shared the inside scoop: another executive from down the hall was nabbed breaking into that safe! We soon parted ways with that customer—we never did receive an apology for their false accusation or a thank-you for the use of our surveillance equipment. It's sad that the janitor usually gets blamed for such instances, but it is understandable since they are often in the buildings at night and have access.

Occasionally we get a call from a customer to report something missing, but instead of an accusation of theft, we are noted for being "too good" at our cleaning. In other words, our cleaners tossed out something that certainly looked like trash and was placed in an area where it naturally would have been assumed to be trash, only it turned out to be something that the customer didn't intend to be taken away and badly needed to be retrieved. Those are the cases when "Detective Gary" is called in to perform his specialty: Dumpster Diving. According to Gary, here is the definition of Dumpster Diving:

Verb; the act of searching through a dumpster to find an item that was mistakenly thrown away. The Good News: if the trash had not been removed by the dumpster services, there was a 95 percent chance the diver could retrieve the missing item(s). The Bad News: Anything retrieved from a Dumpster Dive smelled horrible and the diver usually came away from the experience covered in trash (liquid and otherwise).

The most memorable Dumpster Diving tale will need to be told in the PG-version for inclusion in this book. One morning Gary got a call from an attorney whose office we cleaned informing us that something was missing and insisting that Gary come to the office right away. "So, what's missing?" Gary asked innocently upon his arrival. "Well, you see, it's evidence for a big divorce case coming up, evidence about infidelity." Upon careful questioning, Gary discovered that the evidence was stored in a plastic grocery bag that had been set next to a trash can in the office's break room. Since it was resting next to the trash can, the customer understood why our employee would have thought it was trash, so our employee was in the clear. The contents of that missing bag included a video of a genre that adults in an illicit situation might call upon, an empty liquor bottle, a love note pinned to a pair of ladies' underwear, and an item used for protection during their act of physical union.

Hoping for the best, Detective Gary first checked the janitor closet where our cleaners will sometimes put something "on ice" while making sure it was really meant for the landfill. With no success there, it was down to the back alley where the dumpster contained approximately 12 bags of trash and at least a few rats. Deftly avoiding the rats, Gary maneuvered his way through the trash until uncovering an envelope from the lawyer's office and then, finally, the missing contents outlined in the tossed-out trash bag. One piece of evidence was in especially disgusting condition— you can probably guess which one—and Gary could not locate the video, only the sleeve of the video box. We never did find out how that lawyer's case turned out, but Detective Gary has vivid memories of the long, hot shower he took as soon as he got off duty that day. But to satisfy a customer, it was well worth it for Gary.

Gary could live without being such a top-notch Dumpster Diver, though. The truth is that he'd rather not be brought in for this type of work at all, but when you're running a cleaning business you sometimes have to do the dirty jobs that other companies would never be asked to do. And if you want to persevere, you just put on your gloves and get down to the task at hand.

Speaking of infidelity, you would be amazed at what a janitor may stumble into. We once had another attorney's office that we cleaned and they had a receptionist who could sometimes have some pretty unrealistic expectations regarding the cleaning of their office. She expected it to be cleaned like her home and had no qualms about letting us know about it. That is, until one day things changed. You see, our account manager came by the attorney's office one late night only to discover that receptionist having "relations" with one of the attorneys on the couch. Guess what? We never heard any more complaints.

Going back to our Kmart DC days, we did something else that many entrepreneurs do when their company begins to achieve some success: we began to pursue other business ideas. One of our earliest ventures extended directly out of our business relationship with Kmart. When we noticed their heavy reliance on temp services, we launched our own staffing business, Supreme Staffing, to help them out. That venture lasted only as long as our Kmart DC account. Then, during the period when the "sick building syndrome" had become the talk of our industry, we bought a franchise called Environmental Air Services, which was essentially an air duct cleaning operation. This was a more significant investment, requiring an SBA loan of about $30,000 to purchase equipment and create a TV commercial. Unfortunately, we may have been ahead of our time on that one—our new service never really caught on.

When we were able to get our franchise fee back, we rolled that money into the heating and air industry, partnering with a friend we knew from playing softball. We started a completely sperate business, and since our friend had extensive HVAC experience and we had none, we relied on him to take the lead on operations. That turned out to be a big mistake. After a promising start, the business began losing money and our partner, as evidenced by the scorecards we found in his company car, had apparently been spending a lot of time at the golf course. We got out of the partnership and let him have the business, which only resulted in the unpaid debt landing in our laps. In the end, we lost more than $50,000 there.

SMO was solid enough to absorb the loss, and David walked away with a valuable lesson: never again would he enter into any kind of major business venture with any partner other than Gary. The trust and confidence we had in one another was unparalleled, and we knew that the strength of our partnership was vital to our success. It simply could not be duplicated with anybody else.

This was not the first time that someone we had trusted to do their job fizzled out. We both remember well the first sales person we hired, a fellow we later called "Smoking Joe." This guy impressed us during the interview with his previous experience in drumming up business for other cleaning services he had worked with, and we turned him loose to see what he could produce for us. Six months later, he had produced nothing. After we leaned on him a little, he informed us that he had sold an account that would begin in 30 days. We ordered the equipment, hired an employee and were ready to roll.

David walked into his office on the day we were to start, only to discover Joe's keys and other work materials on his desk. It seemed that this "sale" was fabricated, and Joe had run off. There's a funny ending to this story. Sometime later, we got a call from a gentleman named Allen Lillard who worked for Starmount Company, a very prominent property management company in Greensboro. Mr. Lillard mentioned that they had initially been contacted by old Smoking Joe. We ended up doing a lot of business with Starmount Company and we still do business with some of their key folks today. We joked that maybe we should hunt Old Smoking Joe down and send him a commission check and thank-you note. We learned to be very leery of potential sales people who tell you about all the cleaning contracts they have sold and how much business they can bring in. If they sound too good to be true, they probably are.

Learning how to deal with the occasional individual that drops the ball and dumps a big headache on your lap is just another part of persevering. That was part of the terrain we had to successfully navigate as business owners, and we didn't let the few troublemakers slow us down. Anyway, right from the beginning we were consistently blessed with having the vast majority of those who worked for us prove to be the kind of hard-working and trustworthy men and women that contributed to our growth and success in many positive ways.

That was especially true when we first began hiring our first Spanish-speaking workers. This leads us to the story of another of our side business ventures. Of all these attempts at finding a new business that would either help our company soar or guide us into a totally different industry, this was the one that most appeared primed to take off. Here's how it came about:

We began hiring large numbers of Spanish-speaking employees during our Kmart DC days. Most of them were hard-working, family folks who quickly became a vital part of our staffing. One employee, Concepcion, began serving as our channel into the Spanish-speaking community. When we would tell Concepcion that we needed to hire more people, he would immediately respond, "How many do you need and when do you need them?" Sure enough, the needed cleaners would show up, ready and eager to work. At one point, Spanish-speaking employees made up more than 50 percent of our 150-person workforce.

We were naturally very pleased by the contributions these workers were making, but sometimes we ran into roadblocks trying to communicate with them. Sure, we had both taken Spanish in high school, but as you will recall we did not exactly excel in the classroom. Gary did his best in picking up at least a few key Spanish words and phrases: *mesa* for table; *alfombra* for carpet, etc. His employees taught him much more than school ever did. Sometimes, though, his translations didn't quite click. Once, while he was training a group of female Spanish-speaking employees, he was trying to explain how something only had to be dusted "one time" a week when he happed to call upon the Spanish word *beso* to drive home his point. "Uno beso aqui por semana" Gary proclaimed. This triggered a round of giggles from the trainees, and when Gary asked them what was so funny, they continued to laugh. The next morning Gary told our bilingual receptionist Tina about the previous night. Sure enough, Tina laughed too. "Gary, you were telling them one kiss here per week. Una vez por semana is once per week," Tina stated as she continued to laugh. While Gary also thought it was funny, he knew that the employees appreciated the effort just as much as the accuracy.

Some of our managers didn't speak one word of Spanish. This was a problem not just in explaining the different tasks that their workers needed to perform but also involving issues of safety. One of our ladies got hit by a forklift in an accident on the job at the Kmart DC one day, and as she talked and talked in her attempt to explain her condition, we couldn't understand a word she was saying. We wound up getting her to the hospital and thankfully she was fine, but incidents like that one emphasized the importance of understanding basic words and phrases in Spanish.

The way we figured it, if this was a major problem for us, it was very likely to be a problem for almost any cleaning service, and probably in many other lines of work too. We were going to step in and offer the solution: "Speak Cleaning in Spanish." The idea was to create a software program that would teach people like us industry-specific words and phrases in Spanish to successfully communicate with their Spanish-speaking employees. Managers could print out "cheat cards" to carry with them for immediate use on job sites or around their office.

We went all-in with this venture, even hiring a patent attorney who surprisingly obtained a broad patent that would cover not only programs designed to teach industry-specific terms in Spanish for the cleaning business but for *any* language in *any* industry. We envisioned expanding into the realm of EMTs, doctors, police departments, banking and many other domains. When we first tested the market by introducing our program as exhibitors at industry trade shows in 1999, we quickly became the buzz of the show.

Inspired by this enthusiastic response, we put together a prospectus and decided to incorporate. Calling our business Lingo Solutions, we raised $40,000 in $5,000 shares, two of which were bought by Gary's father. We had also invested about $50,000 of our own to get us to this point. We were convinced that this business would totally change our lives, enabling us to hang up our rags and pour all our time and energy into this exciting high-tech opportunity.

Break the Language Barrier On The Cleaning Worksite With speak cleaning IN SPANISH Patent Pending Software. presented by: Lingosolutions

Speak Cleaning in Spanish brochure

When we look back at that time today, David's wife Paula has been known to wonder out loud what might have happened if the popular TV show *Shark Tank* had been around back then. Oh, we could have made quite a pitch about how our trail-blazing business with the powerful patent was going to revolutionize every industry that had to deal with language barriers...if we could just acquire a little assistance from an investor. We would have told them how we had quickly sold over 100 programs in our industry, and that it only cost us $8 or $10 to make the CDs that we were selling for $300. We have no doubt that we would have attracted one or more offers from the likes of Kevin O'Leary, Robert Herjavec or Mark Cuban. Alas, that's something we'll never know.

But even without that one big backer, the promise of riches that would fulfill David's teenage dreams was dancing in our minds. That's when we decided to put SMO on the market in 2000, so we could use the money from the sale to pour into Lingo Solutions. After attracting interest from potential buyers in our industry, we were steaming head-on toward the biggest decision we ever faced. Should we abandon the 11 years of hard work that had enabled us to employ hundreds of good people while making a decent living for ourselves to chase the pot at the end of the rainbow? Or should we let go of the dream of something bigger and hold tight to what we had? We didn't have the resources to do both because we realized we would need hundreds of thousands of dollars to successfully launch a tech business. We would need to either sell SMO or find some angel investors.

Our top potential buyer was getting serious, with one viable offer on the table and a willingness to negotiate. At that point, we knew that we could not make this decision alone. We decided to drive down to Charlotte and locked ourselves in a room at The Westin Hotel for a few days so that we could pray about this question, to put our faith in God to guide us toward the right course of action. Knowing that we were about to receive the final offer, we said, "Lord, if you want us to sell this business, we want them to make an offer of X. If they don't offer that much, we will accept that as a sign to hold onto SMO and let go of this big dream."

It was January 2001 when that last offer was placed in our hands. Our target sale price was $1,175,000; their offer was $1,145,000. With only a $30,000 difference, we were tempted to just say, "Well, maybe we didn't pray hard enough" or go back to the prospective buyer and negotiate one more time to reach a deal that either landed on our target or came really close to it.

But we knew that we could not do that now. We had asked God for a sign, and He had provided it to us. We were meant to hold on to our cleaning business. We would not be putting down our rags after all. You never regret making a right decision.

Next came Supreme Maids. We had several of our peers tell us how successful they had been in adding the residential cleaning business to their portfolio, so we decided to jump in. We went out and hired a manager to run this new service. We advertised, hired some maids and started providing weekly and bi-weekly maid services throughout Greensboro. We built up a pretty good little book of business after a year or so but as you can probably guess, we were still not turning a profit. We were quickly learning that the residential cleaning business was very different from the commercial cleaning business and SMO was just not cut out for it. So we cut our losses and closed this division down and moved on.

In 2014, after a previous failed attempt, we decided to make a serious effort to establish a commercial landscaping division of SMO. After all, we heard from other building service contractors that the landscape business offers much better margins than the janitorial business. We went out and hired an executive guy with lots of landscape experience to come in and help us build a successful landscape division. Once again, we learned that although there may be some similarities, the landscape business is very different from the janitorial service business. Even though we were able to build it up enough to hire a full landscape crew, we were still losing money after three years. As you can imagine, we had invested quite a bit of money in vehicles, equipment and salaries and were getting close to a break even point, but we made the difficult decision to sell our landscape division in 2017.

After all these experiences, we began to think that maybe all these attempts at launching some kind of side venture or replacement for our cleaning business were just distractions. We invested a lot of money and sweat into making them work, but one after another, they didn't take us where we wanted to go. But we didn't moan about our bad luck, bad timing or our own inability to turn a new vision into something big that we could keep building on. We learned that it's hard to chase two rabbits and get them both. You focus on one, and you make sure you get one. We just buckled down and focused on our bread and butter: Supreme Maintenance Organization.

We certainly don't want to say never, but we have no plans to move into any other businesses unless it's just an absolute no-brainer. We just decided that we were going to do everything we could to soar as high as possible on the wings of our own janitorial service business. After coming close to letting go of SMO in 2000, we should have learned our lesson and stayed focused on our cleaning business. Maybe our growth since then has not been meteoric, but it's been steady. Even during downturns when other companies were laying people off left and right, especially during the 2008-09 economic crisis, we have still been able to grow and employ lots of people. The janitorial service industry is not recession proof, but it is recession resistant. People still need clean working environments even during a down economy.

We are finally starting to learn that we just need to keep doing what we have always done best. Cleaning. After all, we are just a couple of janitors who got together and built up a successful and highly respected janitorial business.

CHAPTER 4

The Right DNA: The People Who Enable SMO to Soar

If there's one thing we have learned ever since we first expanded Supreme Maintenance Organization beyond a crew of a couple of janitors named David and Gary fresh out of college, it is that our people are a major part of our success. Well, that's not exactly right. Our people are really *all* of it—the key component of building a successful and growing company for 30 years and counting. To put it simply, our company is nothing without our people.

Our employees, whom we now more accurately refer to as our "team members", are out there doing all the work that a cleaning service must do to survive and thrive. In our highly-competitive business, the only thing that separates us from our competitors is the quality of our people. When we talk about how we have persevered through all the changes and challenges of running this business, we should always start with the understanding that we have persevered because of our people.

We're up to about 600 team members today, and we could spend at least 600 hours expressing our deep gratitude for those who keep our SMO engine humming. Although we may not have adequate time in this 30-year anniversary story to properly salute all of our people and the contributions they have made to our success, we will try to touch upon some of the highlights here.

Our leadership team in 2014

We'll start with the word that probably best describes most of the people who work for us. That word is *humble*. These are good, honest, hardworking, family-oriented individuals, but humility is the trait that really makes an impression on us. Those who choose to share this dedication to our cleaning business are truly humble, salt-of-the-earth people. We're proud to be a part of the same team with them.

You could say that any man or woman, whether young or old, has to be humble to work in our industry. After all, what we do is often looked upon in some places as acting in a subservient role—we're cleaning up other people's messes. It takes a certain kind of person to be willing to do it, to care about doing it and to commit to doing it consistently over months or, in many cases on our team, for many, many years.

We do everything we can to help our dedicated team members to completely rise above any stigma attached to being "just a janitor." Most anyone who does this work for a living usually comes with a willingness to accept doing what some people might look down on. We still carry memories from our early days running our business when one of our workers would be out on a job site around some of the customer's employees and someone would put their arms around our guy as if to say, "Poor Charlie, he's only a janitor." We know the truth, and the people who work for us understand the truth. The reality is that what we do is extremely important. No business can function without us. We know that we can have a direct impact on our customer's success.

David remembers reading an article about what happened a few years ago when workers at the New York City airports went on strike. With unclean toilets, empty paper towel racks, overflowing trash bins and a bunch of other problems, the scene quickly became chaotic. As everyone discovered, those cleaners were vital to the safe, healthy and comfortable operation of the airports.

So, when our people are out there cleaning a large commercial office building, or a branch office of a trusted bank, or the classrooms, corridors and restrooms of a school, they are creating and maintaining a healthy environment. They play a critical role in the day-to-day activities in those workplaces and places of learning. Yet they're not getting paid high salaries because of the nature of our thin-margin industry, and when they clean empty offices late at night they are often invisible. They do it because they need the money, sure, but they also do it and do it well because they *care.*

It is not unusual for one of us to get a call from a customer singing the praises of one of our Cleaning Technicians for doing something that went above and beyond what was required or expected. As business owners, you'd like to take some of the credit for these kinds of testimonials. After all, we hired and trained these people. But we know that the person who had just been singled out for praise simply came to us with the right DNA. They are the kind of people who will always do an excellent job, often going way beyond what is required, because that is who they are— it's their nature. Over the years, we've been blessed to have had hundreds and hundreds of people who had that right DNA and happened to come work for us.

When we train our team members, we seek to instill a winning attitude toward the work they will perform: you need to have a service hand and a service head, but you need to have a "servant's" heart. It just reflects an approach to cleaning where they understand they are truly serving the important needs of others.

When Gary takes a new group of team members inside a school they will be cleaning, he says, "Look at this classroom. It's empty right now, but every chair in this room represents somebody's son or daughter, brother or sister, niece or nephew. You have the opportunity to have a positive impact on the life of that person that you can't see and don't know."

With a 600-person workforce, there will certainly be some who won't exactly see things that way, who are just there to get a paycheck at a time when it may have been difficult for them to find work. A few workers may be offended by the term "servant." But the comforting reality for us as leaders of SMO is that the vast majority of our people do not even have to be guided into adopting that kind of successful attitude. They already had it, and they will exhibit it every day they work, providing clean and healthy facilities for our customers.

So we're not at all surprised when we get those calls applauding one of our team members for a performance that demonstrates real caring. It might show up in the way a stack of magazines is organized, or the precise arrangement of items on a desk at a work station, or maybe just the willingness of our team member to immediately agree to a request to do something not in their job description, like helping to move a heavy table. With our administrative staff, we can walk into our office on a holiday and find key people catching up on important tasks and details. They're not getting paid any extra to be there on what should be a day off, they're just committed to doing everything they can to help us remain successful.

Sometimes a customer will do more than offer a few words of praise for one of our people. It's not unusual for one of our customers to say something like, "I'm not going to try to tell you how to run your business, but I will tell you that whatever you do, you've got to hang onto the lady who cleans my office every night. She's great!" Some of our day porters, who are more likely to interact with our customers while on the job, share stories with us about the many ways in which customers express their appreciation. One customer gave one of our team members an all-expense-paid cruise. Another customer, upon hearing that the Cleaning Technician who worked in his office was grieving the recent passing of her son in Mexico, offered to buy her a round-trip airline ticket to go to the memorial service. When the drivers around one of the sites of our logistics customer noticed that one of our guys would always arrive for his cleaning shift by taxi or bicycle, they chipped in to buy him a moped. We sometimes laugh that our workers often get more recognition than we do as owners, but we are thrilled that this is the case. Our people deserve all of that and more!

We learned very early in running our business that our emphasis was not going to be on valuing our people just for what they do, but for who they are. Not everyone can perform a cleaning job consistently and well. Other than those welcome stories about customers going out of their way to praise or appreciate a cleaner, this is often a thankless job. As we mentioned in the previous chapter, it can seem like you never hear anything from a customer until that day that somebody misses a trash can. But the people who have the right DNA for this job are not discouraged by that. They just keeping doing a good job, because they care and because it's the right thing to do.

Many of our people will tell you they like the instant gratification that comes with cleaning. When you walk into an office and you find a table that's a real mess, with handprints and food particles all over it, and you throw yourself into the task of cleaning it, you see the change. That table is now all nice and shiny, and you soak in that instant gratification of looking at the evidence of the excellent job you just did. If you approach a beat-up floor with no shine and you proceed to strip and refinish that floor in an efficient and thorough manner that leaves it shining like a new penny, you can't help but feel good.

Now, does that mean our people all go about their cleaning tasks dancing and singing with joy? We wouldn't make that claim, although we do remember one of our cleaners, Hazeline Smith, a former Team Member of the Year, who would softly sing choir music or just hum out loud while she went about her cleaning duties. Other team members have told us they like cleaning because they are able to approach their tasks in kind of a relaxed state, where they allow themselves to think about other important questions and concerns in their lives. Of course, they understand that they have to maintain their focus so that they don't miss that last trash can, but while still doing an excellent job they are able to let go of something else going on that may be stressful to them. That's a lot harder to do in many other jobs.

Another way that we can identify the right DNA in our people is by evaluating the assessment tests that we give our job candidates today. We are always confident in selecting new team members who demonstrate through their assessment that they accept personal responsibility for where they are in their lives. They don't make excuses, point fingers or blame other people or their environment for anything that has happened to them. Instead, they accept that they are responsible for taking the circumstances of their lives and shaping their own destiny. We are also able to identify applicants who demonstrate sustained focus, which is important when performing very monotonous and repetitive tasks. We know that those are the kinds of people that are more likely to do a great job servicing our customers.

Since our team members are out there showing how much they care about the work that they do every day, our job is to show them how much *we* care about *them*. It didn't take us long after launching SMO to develop a deep appreciation for our employees. Remember, we started out with just the two of us doing all the cleaning, but as soon as we began to get regular jobs that required a crew of 10 or 15 people, we would look at each other and say, "Hey, if these people don't come to work tonight, we can't clean all these buildings by ourselves!"

Over the course of 30 years, we have always looked out for as many ways as possible to show our appreciation, support, respect and compassion for those who come to work with us every day. We believe that our internal customers should be #1 to us, ahead of our external customers. We want to do whatever we can to back up that belief. It starts with the company environment and culture that we seek to create and maintain. Even as we have expanded into a professional regional company that extends way beyond a handful of buildings in and around Greensboro, we have tried to keep up a family type atmosphere.

This is something we are proud to share with our new or potential customers. We tell them that we offer the same level of professionalism, the same resources, the same certifications as much bigger janitorial companies, but we're still a family. You don't have to cut through a lot of red tape to deal with us as business owners. We're the guys you will actually talk to, not like some owners who keep themselves one or two steps removed from the actual operation of their company. We're totally hands-on in our approach to leadership.

To our team members who do the work, we try to create an understanding that we are not really in the cleaning business, we're in the customer service business. That's how we hope they will relate to our customers, and that's how we want to relate to them as team members. Our approach toward them sounds something like this:

"You might not get paid as much as you want or as much as we would like to pay you, but we can appreciate you and demonstrate that you are valued and important to us. We are here to serve you because you are part of the SMO family."

That attitude begins with our first-hand understanding of what they do and the challenges that come with professional cleaning. We can honestly say, "We've been there. We've done the work that you're doing. We know how taxing and draining it can be." We also know what it's like to take on the criticism and complaints that can often come with being anything less than 100 percent perfect in your cleaning. We realize that we are only as good as our last performance and we strive for perfection each day. But we know that any time you're dealing with people, there will always be human error. That's especially true in cleaning services, where your one and only mistake is going to be visible and the first thing your customer notices.

When mistakes happen, we try to be empathetic: "Okay, you made a mistake. Now, let's make sure we fix the mistake, try to learn from it and do whatever we can to prevent it from recurring. You missed the break

David, Anthony Oliver and Gary in 1989

room trash can on the third floor, fine, but let's not miss the trash can on the third floor again. Whatever we did to cause the oversight, let's work real hard not to make the same mistake again."

As hands-on owners, when a customer's complaint lands on our lap, it quickly becomes not only the customer's issue but our issue. Our level of concern matches or exceeds the customer's level. In an effort to prevent animosity towards our customers, now the concern comes from our management team and we refrain from saying this customer said this or that. We know the complaint is a way of communication and we use it as an opportunity to become better. We want to protect our frontline cleaners from additional stress and anxiety. Our value of our team members can sometimes exceed our customers and we do not want our team members to lose confidence or become discouraged.

Even in those very rare cases where one of our workers does something seriously wrong, we still try to be compassionate. As we described earlier, customers can be quick to blame the cleaner when something disappears during the night. More often than not, their suspicion proves to be wrong. But there was an occasion when one of our workers was guilty of taking a few sodas from a customer's refrigerator. We had to let him go, of course, but when our manager heard this worker apologize and then explain that he felt he had to steal because he didn't have enough money to feed his family, that manager drove that dismissed team member right to the grocery store and bought him a full load of groceries to take home as a final gesture.

We've had many other situations when one of our folks needed temporary financial help, maybe because their car broke down or some other unexpected expense came up, and we've loaned them money to get through their tough time. If a team member loses his home to a fire, we immediately pitch in and invite others in the company to help out if they choose to do so. One of our managers who had a family member with a disability happened to mention once that this person needed a specific kind of bicycle to ride, and that it would go a long way toward building that child's confidence. The two of us immediately responded with financial help, and we were amazed that some of our team members took a couple hundred bucks out of their own pockets to contribute. That's just the kind of people they are.

The way we figure it, if you are a family and someone in your family hurts, you hurt too. There will always be professional lines that no business owner can or should cross, but in certain times of need you don't draw the line at all. You just put the chalk away and let your compassion lead the way.

We have always believed that to maintain our family atmosphere and build trust and loyalty with our team members, we have to give them a lot more than a paycheck. That means doing things for our people every day, not just when particular needs or problems arise.

As experienced cleaners ourselves, we understood that one way we could support our new team members would be to provide them with real hands-on training. In many cleaning companies, employees are given very little training or direction—you're just handed the supplies and expected to start cleaning. When we hire new team members, they attend SMO University, our own professionally facilitated training program where they learn step-by-step procedures to complete any cleaning task, as well as important instruction regarding safety and security. We want our people to feel fully prepared and confident when they start working on-site. We also provide them with SMO logo navy blue uniforms to wear on the job, so they can feel a greater sense of pride in what they do and carry a reminder that they are part of a team.

Once they begin work, we support them when any challenges or issues arise. In those situations where something disappears and the customer rushes in to blame our team member, we put on the brakes. We resist falling into the trap of assuming guilt and will always stand up for our people until proven guilty. Some business owners in our industry react the opposite way—assuming guilt unless and until innocence is proven. But when you know that your people have the right DNA, and you've worked in the trenches and understand what it feels like to be falsely accused, you have to consistently take a strong stand on behalf of your team members.

We also remind our people regularly that their own families should come first—when something comes up that needs their time and attention, we will work with them to help take care of their scheduling needs. We offer paid vacation time to all our team members, including the part-timers that make up the majority of our workforce, and whenever possible we try to say yes to a team member's request for specific vacation time.

We acknowledge team members for their excellent service through our Team Member of the Month awards and the J.D. Murphy Team Member of the Year Award named after David's father, who worked for us part-time in quality control before he passed away in 2005. We chose to honor his dad in that way because if it were not for Jimmy Murphy and his janitorial service, there probably would not even be a Supreme Maintenance Organization today. We named our first Employee of the Year, the late Peggy Seger, in 1995. At Christmas, we hold an annual turkey give-away for all our team members. That happens at our celebration in Greensboro where we provide a big meal of barbecue, pizza and fried chicken, as well

Gary with
Peggy Seger
at the SMO
office

as a whole turkey to bring home so they can say to their family, "Here, I'm putting meat on the table." For those too far away to make it to Greensboro, we offer gift cards so they can buy their own turkey. That annual celebration also features the "Share Shop," which is like a free yard sale in which team members can take home any of the items they desire. The donated items come from other team members as well as friends, families and customers of SMO.

Team members also have the opportunity to earn what we call SMO Bucks. This is a simple system we modeled from the Green Stamps that we remember from our own childhoods. Our people earn SMO Bucks for excellent attendance, careful adherence to safety standards, staying late on the job when requested, getting a compliment from a customer, and all kinds of other ways in which they demonstrate their commitment and high-level performance. We encourage our managers to creatively look for ways to acknowledge their team members in this way.

When SMO Bucks are accumulated, they can be redeemed for items such as sweatshirts or hats with the SMO logo. SMO Bucks can even earn Walmart gift cards and, ultimately, a paid day off.

Five years ago, we made a special gesture to honor all the people who had contributed to our success by putting together a 25-year anniversary celebration. We tried to go all out for this 100-plus attendee gala. We held the event at the Joseph S. Koury Convention Center, the premier meeting space in Greensboro. We served a full meal, brought in an excellent keynote speaker and entertained everyone there with our big "cake," a gray Rubbermaid Brute trash can with a caddie bag and candy spray bottles. Yes, all us janitors dressed up, and we had a great time recognizing the winner of our J. D. Murphy Team Member of the Year award and presenting gifts to all our 5-year, 10-year and 15-year employees. As we shared the history of our company, with Gary doing most of the talking because he's better at that than David, we also took a moment for the two of us to receive what we call our "Super Bowl" rings in recognition of our roles in launching our business and keeping it humming for 25 years.

Each year we hold our Team Member Awards and Recognition Banquet where we recognize all of our Team Member of the Month winners, team members who have reached milestone anniversaries are presented

Murphy & Collins families at 25th Celebration in 2014

with gifts chosen from our recognition catalog, and we announce our J.D. Murphy Team Member of the Year. Today, our J.D. Murphy Team Member of the Year receives a nice plaque and $1,000 cash. We still get ribbed from some of our previous Team Members of the Year because back in the day they only got about $300 and a limo ride. This is our opportunity each year to roll out the red carpet and show our team members in a small way how much we appreciate them and all they do for our customers.

Today, at our 30-year mark, we have another opportunity to look back and acknowledge team members who have served us through their long-term commitments. Although we must keep a lean administrative staff, we've always tried to provide opportunities for growth for proven and valued team members. To name a few, Al Summers came to work part-time for us after retiring from a successful military career. After his stint as third-shift supervisor with the Kmart DC job, he went on to become Account Manager, Human Resources Manager and now a District Manager. Al was one of the two team members that we took aside after we lost the Kmart DC account to assure them that they would stay on with us.

Ken Allen, our old neighborhood buddy from childhood who helped Mr. Murphy out on those all-night jobs, began with us as a part-time bookkeeper and earned his way to the position of Corporate Controller. David likes to say of Ken, "I trust him with my money, my wife and my life."

Duryea "Juice" Taylor started out as a part-time Cleaning Technician, and after promotions to Site Supervisor and then Account Manager, he has settled in as our Quality Assurance Manager. With his consistently positive attitude, his energy and his enthusiasm, Juice is very popular with both internal and external customers.

Diana Wilson joined us back in 1996, taking a chance by accepting the job of Office Manager even though she initially found our office environment in our former office on Westgate Drive "a little sketchy." As she remembers her growth trajectory, David soon began making invitations like, "Why don't you start making calls to potential clients for me? Why don't you come with me when I go visit this potential customer? Why don't I show you how to do a proposal? Why don't you start doing sales?" Diana just kept saying yes, and she earned her way to the position of Vice President of Business Development as our first non-owner on the executive team. She says she appreciates the SMO family atmosphere and values David's sincere and authentic mentoring, and Gary's caring and forgiving nature. To us, the only reason we've been able to maintain a family atmosphere is because of people like Diana who care about their work and keep showing up to help the team.

Shanda Everett started with us in 2001 as a part-time Sales Assistant. Today, she is our Office Manager. Shanda is the glue who holds us all together and we could not imagine that we would be where we are today without her hard work and dedication. It is not at all unusual to find her at the office after hours or on the weekend. As a parent of a special needs child it is amazing that she manages to get it all done.

We try to find opportunities for anyone who does an excellent job and

David & Gary recognizing Diana for 20 years' service

seeks more responsibility. We remember the example of Steve Gardner, who had been with another company before coming to work for us part-time as a Cleaning Technician. When we noticed that Steve's level of care was extraordinary, he was promoted to Supervisor and then Account Manager. Steve has stuck with us for over 20 years and still works on a part-time basis as a Trainer. He now runs his own cleaning business and we have helped him out by providing job leads and some subcontracting opportunities.

We would like to mention four other long-term team members who have been with us for twenty years. Jesus Fonseca is an Account Manager at one of our largest accounts and has been crucial in the growth and longevity of this valued customer. He first started with us in 1997 as a Cleaning Technician at our Kmart DC job and quickly worked his way into a position of leadership. Etta Tweedy, Site Supervisor, Paul Cathcart, Site Supervisor, and Leroy "Rookie" Haywood, Floor Technician all started with us in 1999.

Interesting story about Rookie: in 1999 we landed a multi-building contract for a local property management company that had their own cleaning staff. Part of the deal was that SMO would retain their crew. Gary and David met with the crew a few days before the start date to introduce themselves and SMO. Then the two met with each crew member individually to discuss pay rates and other details. The meeting with Rookie was a little intense, and after the meeting David told Gary that that "this guy wouldn't last two weeks." Well, here he is twenty years later still doing a great job serving our customers and keeping their floors shinning. So much for David's career as a prognosticator.

We would have to also recognize our longest tenured team member, Marlene Lash. Marlene has been a Cleaning Technician with us since 1995. She comes to work with a smile on her face every day and has been tasked with cleaning the SMO Corporate offices. Sometimes the highlight of our day is getting to cut up with Marlene while she cleans our office.

As we have expanded, we have rolled along through many changes in the way that we engage with our team members. It wasn't all that long ago that our local employees would show up at our office door to receive their paychecks every other Friday. That was a great way to maintain contact with everybody until the expanded numbers of team members and the wider geographical territory we covered, as well as changes in technology, led us to shift to electronic payments. We always look to practice ways to keep our people engaged, whether they work on a team of 10 to 15 cleaners or they perform their cleaning tasks on an island as "Site Supervisor," meaning they clean and supervise a site alone. Our managers work diligently at making sure those team members feel supported and valued.

As part of our commitment to engaging our team members, we also do everything we can to support and engage our managers, whether they work directly out of our Greensboro office or in one of our other locations in North Carolina, Virginia or South Carolina. We like having our managers come to Greensboro monthly for team meetings and training. We also hold weekly conference calls with our operation managers to review account particulars. That's one more way for us to keep the family atmosphere alive.

No matter what systems or procedures we maintain, the most effective approach to showing our team members that we value them is by doing the "little" things. In our main office on Wendy Court in Greensboro, where we have been operating since 2010, Gary has a routine of looking through the office pile of outgoing mail. When he recognizes the name of one of the recipients of mail heading out of SMO, he picks up the envelope, turns it over and hand-writes a personal message on the back: "Thank you for all your help, you're the best!" or "What's up, my man Alberto?" We're not sure what the post office thinks about this little gesture, but it works for us. It's one of those practices that simply says. "We care."

Of all the feedback we receive from the many people involved with the operations of Supreme Maintenance Organization, we can easily point to the greatest compliment anyone can ever give us. That is when one of our team members says, "Working for SMO is like working for a family."

CHAPTER 5

Four Industry Leaders Share Their Success Stories

A s we have pointed out, our story of rags to riches is not all that unusual, especially in the cleaning industry. To help illustrate this point, we are now going to feature brief profiles of leaders from four other cleaning businesses with whom we have a special relationship.

These four companies are members of our Peer Group. You see, we get together at each location and audit each other's businesses on a regular basis. We teleconference monthly to share ideas and to seek advice on any specific issues we may have going on at the time. Our group has an open book policy and, because we are not competing directly with each other, we can feel free to share openly. The five companies have a combined revenue of over $50 million and employ thousands of dedicated service workers. Our Peer Group has been an invaluable resource and has become part of our SMO extended family.

In reading these profiles, one thing that you will quickly notice is that just like SMO, each business was started with little to no resources but has grown into an industry leader. None of the founders was born with a sliver spoon or graduated in the top of their class from Harvard. Most did not necessarily have a ton of business experience when starting out. However, each one of them has worked extremely hard in a very competitive business to achieve success.

Another common theme that you will find in these profiles is that one should never underestimate the complexities of running a cleaning business. Although the barriers to entry are low, which is one reason why this is such a great industry, it's a lot more complicated than just emptying trash cans and cleaning toilets. Building a successful cleaning business requires a lot of grit and determination as you deal with many people, both employees and customers, with different wants, needs and expectations. So, sit back and learn some terrific insights from four of the cleaning industry's best.

The Ups and Downs of Being a Business Owner: *The Story of Clean Team, Inc.*

Bob Armbruster, President

Name of Business: Clean Team, Inc.
Location: Toledo, Ohio
Year the Business Launched: 1996
Locations/Geographic Areas Served: The Midwest and Florida

How did you get started in the cleaning business?
Fresh out of high school in Toledo, I had a job selling magazine subscriptions and happened to make a call on a guy in Detroit who had just started a cleaning service. He told me that he was getting $25 an hour to clean, which in 1995 was big money to an 18-year-old! Over the next several months (and yes, I did sell him the magazine subscription), I picked his brain and put together a very loose plan to start my own cleaning company in Toledo. I printed up some business cards, walked down the street and just started knocking on doors. The people at the second door I knocked on let me give them a quote for cleaning their office, and I said $105 a week. I'm not sure how I came up with $105, but they went for it. Mind you, at that point I didn't know anything about cleaning. So I went home, raided my mom's laundry room closet and grabbed the Comet, her vacuum and whatever looked like cleaning chemicals. "Mom, can you show me how to clean a bathroom?" I asked. I was on my way!

Clean Team crew in 2008

The truth is, I never thought I would make a career out of running my cleaning service. I figured it would just be something I would do for awhile until something else came along. College was not a consideration, even though my father practically begged me to pursue my education. I was just not a classroom kind of guy. But I was determined to learn what I needed to know to make this business work, and with a big lift from my experiences with BSCAI, I really did make a go of it.

What do you like best about running a cleaning business?
It's fast-paced and has unlimited growth potential. My brother Jim, who is 13 years younger than me, joined the company four years ago and is our Vice President. I really enjoy working with him.

What are the major challenges that you have faced and how have you handled them?
Growing pains. You hit certain levels where you find that what you are currently doing won't work in the future. You have to learn to adjust and re-tune. I call it the plateaus of growth.

What is the most difficult thing about operating a cleaning business?

It would surprise most people who are not in our industry, but this is one of the most challenging and complex businesses to run, in spite of it being such a simple concept (it's just cleaning, right?). Also, the janitorial business is all labor, so you're always dealing with different personalities, different wants and needs, and communication challenges that come in working with non-English speaking employees and all different types of individuals.

Cleaning people can be sensitive, and with good reason. They perform a tough and dirty job that most of us wouldn't want any part of, and then we expect them to be perfect and never miss anything. Cleaning people rarely hear the good. Most of the time our communication with them is regarding an issue or complaint. You have to be very careful with the way you communicate with the cleaning staff so as not to offend them.

Example: "I cleaned 75 toilets tonight, and two of them had poop—yes I said poop—on the seat, toilet tank and floor, not to mention the booger wall I had to clean. (Believe it or not, most offices have a stall in the restroom where people wipe their boogers!) And you are upset with me because I forgot to fill one soap dispenser?!"

Who has helped you most along the way, and what is the best advice you ever received?

My dad was a great coach in life and in business. He worked for 7 Up when I was a kid and would never allow us to drink anything other than 7 Up, until he went to work for Coca-Cola and then all we could drink were Cokes. He taught me the importance of being loyal to your brand and taking pride in your product or service. He also taught me the block and tackle approach: just keep doing what works over and over and over again, have a plan and stick to it. Most people are too impatient to follow these principles.

What have been the biggest moments or major turning points you have experienced?

Joining BSCAI (Building Service Contractors Association International), joining our Peer Group, working with a consultant in the industry and forming a Board of Advisors.

How do you stay motivated and keep your team motivated?
You have to remember why you got into business in the first place. Then you have to realize if it was easy, everyone would be doing it. I set goals and have our Peer Group and our board hold me accountable. I said a long time ago, if we have a year where we don't grow, it's time to sell. Motivating a team has its challenges. It starts by putting together the right team and taking off the handcuffs.

How do you go about making significant decisions?
I'm a big list guy. I like to list all the good, the bad and the ugly. Then I think about it non-stop for days.

How do you manage the stress that comes with owning a cleaning business?
Eat healthy, balance time between work and family, and have a drink now and then!

What book title or two-word phrase would best describe your journey in running a cleaning business?
Title: "Bipolar, The Ups and Downs of Being a Business Owner."

How has operating a successful cleaning business impacted you in other areas of your life?
It's afforded me a lifestyle and the freedom that most people don't have. Since I started with nothing, I appreciate everything that my family and I get to enjoy because of this business.

If you were to identify one benefit or advantage of owning a cleaning business as opposed to other small businesses, what would it be?
The obvious reason most people including myself chose this business is the low cost of entry. Another reason is that it's somewhat recession resistant. Offices, schools, medical and manufacturing facilities are always going to need cleaning, even in a bad economy. They might scale back a

little, but they can't completely cut all janitorial services. Another benefit is that it can't be outsourced. The dirt is in the United States and can't be outsourced overseas.

Also, our industry is made up of a lot of small and unprofessional companies. If you run a professional company, you can be light years ahead of the competition. Huge advantage!

What are your most important goals for the future?
Our 15-year goal is $100 million in revenue.

A Herky-Jerky Ride:
The Story of Encompass Onsite
Marcell Haywood, Chief Executive Officer

Name: Encompass Onsite
Location: Fort Lauderdale, Florida
Year the Business Launched: 2004

How did you get started in the cleaning business?
When I was a college student at Florida State University, I met a guy who was with a building service contracting company. He shared with me that it had afforded him a really good life and had given him a chance to do great things for the people that were part of his organization. I was a student-athlete on the Florida State basketball team, and when I looked at a teammate and partner of mine at the time who had an ice pack on his knee while I had one on my elbow, we figured we couldn't play basketball forever. So we set out on a mission to build a services business in Tallahassee. Not many student-athletes were trying to do things in an entrepreneurial fashion, so maybe we were a little bit ahead of our time.

We were fortunate enough to grow a small operation there to about 75 employees by cleaning rental properties when students would head out of town on winter breaks. We would repaint, replace carpets, do whatever work was needed. Eventually, my partner, who was about five inches taller

Encompass' first van

than I was, did have an opportunity to go on and play basketball professionally and left me with the business. I had focused on the business side and he had focused on operations, and I knew I couldn't handle it all on my own. So I moved back to Fort Lauderdale and hired a couple of fantastic ladies who taught me the nuts and bolts of this type of business from the ground floor up.

What do you like best about running a cleaning business?
The people we have an opportunity to influence and create opportunities for. That's very exciting to me. The individuals who work in the building services industry really are the most salt of the earth type people. Folks like David and Gary and myself get an incredible joy out of knowing these people and giving them a legitimate opportunity to create a career or provide extra income when they need it.

What are the major challenges that you have faced and how have you handled them?
The inherent economics of this business. It's a commodity driven business and most companies compete on price. As a consequence, we can't always pay people what we would want to pay them, and we can't always match their 401 K or give them all the incredible benefits that we think they

deserve. That's the challenge, the downside of this work. But as with any challenge there are enormous opportunities. Most companies in this industry don't handle employment particularly well. For conscious-minded employers, there's a great opportunity to create a better experience for the people that choose to grow their careers in their companies.

What has been the biggest surprise for you in running a cleaning business?

How complex it really is. When we were starting out, we thought, wow, this is a very simple business to operate. Once you get into it, you realize how much complexity there really is. There are complexities layered on top of complexities. I did not anticipate that.

Who has helped you most along the way, and what is the best advice you ever received?

The list of people who have helped me in an important way is probably 40 or 50 names long, so I'm not able to mention them all here except to say that I am forever grateful for their guidance and assistance. One of the best pieces of advice regarding leadership that I have received is about meeting people where they are. I always thought that was a profound approach to understanding the important tenets of leadership. Most leaders stand and pound on their podium and say, "Follow me!" The more effective approach is to meet every individual exactly where they need to be met and then try to lead them to a better place.

How do you stay motivated and keep your team motivated?

I stay motivated just trying to grow our business and be responsible to our customers. That keeps me getting up at 6:30 in the morning every day, staying focused on our mission and our vision.

How do you go about making significant decisions?

I've got a phenomenal team. We do most of our decision-making by consensus and then we have a secondary philosophy that says "disagree and commit," which means that if we can't reach that consensus, someone has to break the tie and everyone has to rally around that decision.

How do you manage the stress that comes with owning a cleaning company?

I tend to just put my head down and try to hammer through stressful times. There's always going to be a level of stress in this business that you can't avoid. All of us have probably become a little bit numb to that first level of stress, but when things really start to pick up, I just try to put my head down and power through it. Occasionally I get out of town and unplug the phone and do something out in nature, maybe in the Bahamas, or the Florida Keys or Colorado, depending on the time of year.

What book title or two-word phrase would best describe your journey in running a cleaning business?

"Herky-jerky." It's definitely not a smooth ride. It's a fun and incredibly rewarding ride but it's certainly not smooth. However, I would add that to know it is to love it. That herky-jerky ride is probably one of the reasons I love the industry so much.

How has operating a successful cleaning business impacted you in other areas of your life?

I don't know that successful is a factual description, but running this business has definitely helped me to be more in-tune with people. I think one of my strengths now is understanding people and communicating well with them. We work in an industry where whether you are genuine or not really matters, which I have learned while trying to build the company day in and day out.

If you were to identify one benefit or advantage of owning a cleaning business as opposed to other small businesses, what would it be?

The flexibility. You don't have to show up at the office every day, because you can really do the work from anywhere. Another major benefit is the satisfaction that comes from engaging with people on the employee side and the customer side.

What abilities or characteristics does anyone need to launch and grow a successful cleaning business?

Wherewithal. They have to be able to power through tough moments without a loss of momentum or enthusiasm.

What are your major goals for the future?
Our BHAG, or Big Hairy Audacious Goal (the term proposed by James Collins and Jerry Porras in their book *Built to Last*), is to create 1,000 better jobs for service professionals. We think that every job in our organization is a better job compared to what that individual would find working somewhere else, especially with one of our competitors. So we want to do what we do at a very high level for thousands of people, not just the folks that are part of our team currently.

A Humbling Journey:
The Story of SMI Facility Services
Val Garcia, President

Name: SMI Facility Services

Location: Albuquerque, New Mexico

Year the Business Launched: 1992

Number of Employees: 250

Locations/Geographic Areas Served: New Mexico, Arizona, Texas, Colorado

How did you get started in the cleaning business?
My dad, who was a pastor, worked on the side as a custodian because he loved doing this type of work. I used to help him buff the hallway floors and sweep the classrooms. But just like David Murphy with his dad, I never wanted to be a custodian myself. I started out as an auto mechanic because I had a love for cars. I was a good mechanic but after awhile, my finger nails were dirty and my knuckles were all banged up and I decided, nah, that's not what I want to do. I decided to get into painting, remodeling and light construction and started a small business in Texas for awhile, but I sold that business and moved to Albuquerque, New Mexico in 1987.

Val & Steve Garcia, circa 1995

That's when I went to work for a building service contractor where I learned different aspects of the business. In three years, I went from supervisor to the branch director.

In 1992, the business owner decided to relocate the business office to Arizona. When he told me that he was going to move the business, I decided to head off on my own. I started cleaning a couple of small buildings, with the help of my wife and kids, and we soon added a couple more buildings. I made a friend that worked in facility management for what is now Century Link. He gave me my first opportunities to bid on other buildings around the state. We got the work and I hired my first few employees. That's when I decided to bring in my brother Steve to help me, and we just continued to grow. We grew from a couple of accounts to half a million dollars of business very quickly. We found ourselves beating our goal of reaching $1 million in revenue in our first five years by reaching that level in two years.

What do you like best about running a cleaning business?
Most people don't realize that cleaning is such a big industry. They think it's just a mop and bucket and dumping the trash. That's also what I

thought. For me, when I attended my first BSCAI convention in Anaheim, California in '89 and saw hundreds of contractors, I was blown away! That's when I really fell in love with the industry.

I really enjoy making things happen. I enjoy seeing how we can take a dirty building and transform it into a clean and beautiful building. I enjoy getting a call in the morning from the building contact praising how great our employees are and how clean their building looks.

Also, you can provide a lot of people jobs. These are people that work hard. For some, it is a second job to help them supplement their income. For others, this is their primary job.

What are the major challenges that you have faced and how have you handled them?
Government regulations. The affordable health care act was really difficult and still is, even as it's changed.

What's the most difficult thing about operating a cleaning business?
Finding service workers. Some just won't clean bathrooms or do certain things. It's gotten a little better but it's still a challenge.

Who has helped you most along the way, and what is the best advice you ever received?
I don't have a college business degree, but I've gained a lot of experience by running my business. I've had many great teachers, and the Peer Group that we started with David and Gary at SMO has been amazing!

Working with my brother Steve has definitely helped me. You hear so many comments about how family companies turn out to be a disaster, but for Steve and me it has worked well. We are 14 years apart. In the beginning, it was like he was more my son than my brother. As we've gotten older, we've grown more into a brother relationship and have become really good partners. We have lunch three or four times a week, we travel to seminars together, and we talk business all the time. We sometimes disagree but we have the same goals and we think the same. It has been a real blessing having Steve at my side. I trust him with everything—I have no doubts about what he does and why he does it. He has also put a lot of trust in me.

What have been the biggest moments or major turning points you have experienced?

With Steve being on the Board of Directors of BSCAI, he has been able to build strong relationships with owners of national companies who have provided us with subcontracting opportunities. These companies know that if you want to do work in New Mexico, it's the Garcia boys you've got to call!

How do you stay motivated and keep your team motivated?

It doesn't take much for me, I love what I do. We do a lot of work on the golf course, and who doesn't get motivated playing golf? Also, we take our management teams to as many BSCAI functions as possible. They come back fired up and ready to make things happen.

How do you go about making significant decisions?

Sleepless nights, a lot of time praying and seeking guidance. My dad was our spiritual leader and from him I learned that you can be honest, run a straight ship, and still be successful. Being raised a Christian, I also knew that I needed to seek a higher power. I never believe I've brought a business to this height on my own. Since we decided that God was going to be our guiding force, He has been helping us at every step of the way.

What book title or two-word phrase would best describe your journey in running a cleaning business?

"Humbling Journey." When I tell people about my upbringing, they don't believe me. They assume I went to college and have a college education. Little do they know that I have a GED because I never finished high school. My parents were very poor. I had to quit school to work and help my parents. Growing up in Texas in the 1960s, we faced a lot of prejudice. I remember being in first grade, when I knew very little English, and I got paddled for speaking Spanish. I didn't know anyone in our family or friends who had gone on to college and became really successful. So I never thought I would either.

In my 20s, I really struggled. There were times when I didn't have any work. People from our church would bring us food because we didn't have money for groceries. After making a conscious decision that I was not going to live like this anymore, I launched my first business. So I went from not having anything to being where I am today. Not having to worry about feeding my family and providing very well for them has been very humbling.

How has operating a successful cleaning business impacted you in other areas of your life?

Being successful in this business has allowed me to make a great living and also be giving to people who are less fortunate. I was also able to provide for my parents when they were still with us for the last 15 years of their lives. My parents were living on a small Social Security retirement check, so I bought them a home and helped them live a very comfortable life. My dad used to tell me, "The more you give, Son, the more you will receive back," and it has been so true. I've been able to give back to the community and provide jobs to help people when they're in need. There was an employee who needed a $500 loan. I went to the bank and got $500 from my account to give to him. A week later, he came back with five crisp $100 bills, and as he teared up he said, "You don't know the bind you got me out of." He thanked me and I handed the bills back to him and told him, "I want you to keep the money to help you and your family." Being able to help someone when they are in need is payback for when I needed help and others helped me.

What abilities or characteristics does anyone need to launch and grow a successful cleaning business?

It takes a lot of stamina at the beginning when starting any business. I used to work what seemed like 24-hour days sometimes. In the early days there were many times when I got a door slammed in my face, but I knew that I had to go to the next door and do it again. I've helped three other people start a janitorial services company, but only one is still around. The others just didn't have that stamina. You've got to be really thick-skinned. Be loyal to your employees and your staff. You've got to understand how to manage people who work for you and take care of them. Believe that they will then take care of you.

What are your most important goals for the future?
I hope to continue growing my business and someday, eventually, I will probably sell it and retire. But for now, I hope to continue providing great jobs for my employees and great service to my customers.

Starting from the Bottom:
The Story of Woodley Building Maintenance
Tiffany Woodley, Chief Financial Officer

Name: Woodley Building Maintenance

Location: Kansas City, Missouri

Year the Business Launched: 1969

Number of Employees: 900

Locations/Geographic Areas Served: Throughout the Midwest

How did you get started in the cleaning business?
Our business was launched by my parents, Jimmy Woodley and Robery Woodley. My dad, who founded our business back in 1969, passed away in 2013. My mother is still active in the business as CEO. Today, my brother Terry and I are both involved. He is Chief Operations Officer and I am Chief Financial Officer. We both grew up around the business, working over summers and school breaks.

My dad grew up in Mississippi, but when he realized that there would be no opportunities for him there in the Jim Crow South, he moved to Kansas City at age 18 because his sister lived there. He was really outgoing, and his personality, along with his tireless commitment, took him a long way. Anyone who met my dad would always say that he never met a stranger. He started cleaning buildings part-time in the evenings to supplement his income from his day job with a vending machine company. When the company went on strike, he amped up his janitorial work and began to see that there were a lot of opportunities in this industry. At first,

Jimmy Woodley, founder of WBM, with his first manager and receptionist, circa 1975

he was doing much of the work himself, with a couple of college students helping him out part-time. My mother, who worked as a hospital dietician, would do the accounting and bookkeeping in the evenings. They were strictly running the business out of their home at that time.

When my dad was called back to work by that vending company, he decided not to go—he would invest all his time and energy into seeing if he could make a go of it with his business. He was cleaning mostly office space and small industrial plants in Kansas City, and then he got an opportunity to bid his first large job, a high-rise building for AT&T. He was the successful bidder but did not have the financial wherewithal to make payroll for a job of that size, and banks were not willing to lend money to small start-up businesses. Fortunately, he obtained a loan from his former boss, a man who had taken a liking to my dad and who often gave him odd jobs at his residence. From then on, he was on his way. My mother was right there with him from the beginning, working for the business while raising my brother and me.

As a kid, I spent hours and hours down at the office, doing any task my parents gave me: opening the mail, helping to clean the office, answering the phone, filing and later assisting with payroll and other responsibilities. My brother worked around the warehouse or out in the field on construction cleaning jobs. I went on to earn a degree in accounting and worked for an accounting firm for awhile, but in 2000, when my dad was dealing with an illness, I asked myself this question: "What do you want to see happen in your life?" Well, a lot of family businesses don't make it to the second generation, and I knew that I had something to offer.

What do you like best about running a cleaning business?
I like the fact that I really believe that however much effort I put into it, I am able to reap even greater rewards—not only financial rewards but just the satisfaction of building something and seeing it grow. I like to be able to make decisions and not have to take months or years to implement something, which you might find in corporate America.

What's the most difficult thing about operating a cleaning business?
Sometimes you feel you are spread really thin. You come in with a plan for the year or that month of what you want to achieve, and you get so caught up in the day-to-day routine of putting out fires that you don't get to work on your long-term plans as much as you would like.

What has been the biggest surprise for you in running a cleaning business?
People are always a surprise! They bring a lot of different things to the table—some of it great, some challenging. It always amazes us when people tell us their grandparent, parent or uncle has worked for our company over the years. Every day is different because our business is so people focused. At the same time, that's what keeps this work interesting. I get to work at 8 or 8:30 and I look up and it's noon, time for lunch, and I look up again and it's time to go home. I'm never bored.

Who has helped you most along the way, and what is the best advice you ever received?

Both of my parents and my grandparents always stressed taking pride in your work. I really try to make sure that we always display a high level of professionalism where our company is concerned. It becomes very personal when it's your name out there. However, I benefit from the fact that I work with family members. When things become stressful, we are able to rely upon one another.

My dad used to say, "If you want to be successful, find something you like to do so you will put the required time and effort into it." He loved this industry, worked right up until the end. He put a lot of time into building the business. He didn't have hobbies—he didn't golf, he didn't go to the movies and seldom took time off, although he would go to the Super Bowl every year.

What have been the biggest moments or major turning points you have experienced?

When you lose the founder of your business, there is obviously a great personal loss. We also wondered about the employees—would they continue to be loyal to the company and could we maintain that feeling of being a real family business? Well, here we are five years out from that loss, and we have retained most of our employees and customers and have made a pretty smooth transition. It helped that the core family members were already working here.

We've worked hard to maintain that spirit of being a family business. Despite growing to a fairly large size, we're very accessible to our clients and our employees. Some people who work out in the field call directly to my office, and I answer the phone. We try to stay visible in the community, too, supporting different causes because a lot of them are organizations that benefit the people who work for us.

How do you stay motivated and keep your team motivated?

Going to our industry association conferences and our Peer Group meetings rejuvenates me. When I see companies that are bigger than ours, I remember that I can work just as hard and I'm just as smart, so there's no reason we can't do it too. I'm also motivated by taking something that my parents started and wanting to build upon that legacy. My mother stepped into the role of Chief Executive Officer after my father passed and provides the leadership and experience to grow the company.

What book title or two-word phrase would best describe your journey in running a cleaning business?
"Starting from the Bottom." My dad was young, he was black, he had a high school education, he had no money, and despite all those things he had the audacity to believe that he could still build something successful. Most people wouldn't have even tried.

How has operating a successful cleaning business impacted you in other areas of your life?
My friends now come to me looking for problem-solving or leadership. One friend whose company had been bought out decided to leave and build her own business, but she didn't have the money to get started. She showed me her business plan, I showed it to my dad, he showed it to someone who invests in start-ups, and she got her business off the ground. She gained an investor and a business adviser. She recently sold that business through a profitable transaction.

If you were to identify one benefit or advantage of owning a cleaning business as opposed to other small businesses, what would it be?
It's a low-barrier entry—you don't need millions of dollars or expensive equipment to get started. However, you do need to put the time in. People who don't know anything about the industry sometimes make the mistake of thinking it's easy—you just sweep and mop and clean toilets. They don't realize how much time and energy go into it, or the level of professionalism and technical expertise that exists within the industry.

What are your most important goals for the future?
Well, we are approaching our 50-year anniversary. We have talked about what we will do to commemorate that but don't have any firm plan yet. It's important because how many businesses make it to 50 years? Mostly, I just want to continue to help our team provide for themselves and their future. We want to let our community know that we will continue to support it as it has us for 50 years.

CHAPTER 6

Guided by Our Faith and Values

A nyone who visits our website (www.smoworks.com) will find an important statement about who we are and how we seek to live our lives and guide our business as soon as they open up the link for our Core Values. They will notice the first value named:

Honor GOD in all that we do.

We make no secret of the fact that we are both Christians. Some time ago we made the decision to dedicate our business to God. That commitment shifted our perspective by helping us realize who our employer really is. Everything that we have accomplished with Supreme Maintenance Organizations is not because of us; it is because of God. He has had His hand in it the whole time, and we would not be here without Him. We have had many close calls over the years when we needed a big check to come in to allow us to meet our obligations, and He always provided an answer to our prayers. Recognizing that our ownership resides in a Higher Power gives us a greater responsibility to find ways to use our business to serve.

We have followed our own individual paths to our faith. David accepted Christ when he was young. Gary did not grow up in a Christian home, but he experienced a moment in his 20's that completely changed his life. It was Easter time, and he happened to be staying at his family's spot in PirateLand, the popular campground on the south end of Myrtle Beach. While attending the Easter sunrise service that morning, Gary was struck by the beauty of the ocean and the power and magic of the word of God being spoken. He had been to church off and on through the years, but suddenly it was as if he were hearing The Word for the first time. The following Sunday, he accepted Christ during the service at 16th Street Baptist Church, where David was a member and where we played youth softball and basketball, and was baptized that night. Gary explains the change in his life this way:

"I feel as if God is with me every day. He has already gone ahead of me and made visions of what will unfold. When I am confronted by difficulties now, I am better able to say 'I can't wait to see what God's going to do with this.' We're all human, we all have our up and down days, but ultimately I rely on my faith to get me through because I know that through Christ, all things are possible."

David reads a couple of chapters of his Bible and prays every morning and finds that his faith enables him to maintain a grounded perspective about the fortunes of SMO. As he describes the importance of his faith, "If I found out one day that we were losing our two biggest customers, would I be stressed? Yes, but then I would turn to my faith in God and I know that would get me through it, and that everything would be okay."

We both remember those long nights when our doubts would creep up and we would find ourselves saying things like, "God, show us what we need to be doing here because we're a couple of college graduates cleaning toilets and we don't know how long we can keep doing this." And then God, in one way or another, would show us once again that we were meant to be doing just what we were doing, and that it was all going to turn out well.

We have both been involved in our Greensboro churches. David and his wife Paula taught Sunday school at Cornerstone Baptist Church while his kids were younger, and Gary coaches youth basketball and programs the lights during services at Lawndale Baptist Church. With our corporate sustainability program, it is our goal to donate 10 percent of our company profits to our churches and other non-profit organizations.

In our roles as co-founders, we strive to walk the walk as Christians as best as we can. Many of our team members know that we are Christians and that we try to run our business accordingly. However, we certainly are not out there hitting anybody over the head with the Bible. We are always respectful about the personal and private choices regarding one's faith. We've had team members who may have been Buddhists or Muslims or Jehovah's Witnesses or followers of some other religious or spiritual tradition. We respect, love and treat them all the same way.

At the same time, we notice that many like-minded people gravitate toward our business. When members of our staff who happen to be Christians are facing personal struggles or challenges in their life, it's not unusual for other Christians in the workplace, including the two of us, to reach out to them and tell them that we are praying for them. And if someone who was not a Christian when they began working for us winds up accepting Christ because of their experience with our company, we are certainly thankful for any role God provided us.

We are consistently motivated to grow and sustain our success as a company because we know that we are providing opportunities for people who work for us. That's one way we have been able to use our business to serve God, which is what our former employee John was reminding Gary when he urged him not to yield to the temptation to quit. Even for front-line cleaners whose opportunities for advancement may be limited, having a job at SMO may be the only work they are able to find at some point in their lives. For our many part-time team members who hold other jobs, the extra income they earn from working for SMO may contribute toward money for college or supplement retirement income. We remember the husband and wife team, Bobby and Carriellen Lloyd, who worked a few hours per night for us after completing their responsibilities at their full-time jobs during the day. They shared with us their motivation: they were calling upon the pay they received from SMO to tithe to their church, something they had not been able to afford to do previously. Their example of sacrifice and giving often serves as a reminder today for us both. In fact, David keeps a program from Bobby's funeral (he passed in 1999) in his drawer to help him remember their sacrifices.

Our faith also has been a contributing factor in our commitment to give back to our community. During Christmas season, we join in the Salvation Army bell-ringing campaign to raise money for toys and necessities for the needy. We also help out at the Salvation Army toy shop and we've regularly participated in the local Adopt a Street program. Cleaning a street comes naturally to a couple of life-long janitors and our crew!

For David, the commitment to the Salvation Army Boys & Girls Club led him down another avenue of giving. Along with his wife, Paula, and his four children—Melanie, Michelle, Mark and Montana—he launched Kids to the Coast, a non-profit organization that sponsors trips to the ocean for kids who have never been to the beach or only rarely get to go there.

The idea actually was born when we were coaching youth baseball together during our college days at Elon. When we brought an all-star team to compete in a tournament in Virginia Beach, David was amazed to see several kids from the team run and plunge into the ocean water with their clothes on. Those kids had never been to the ocean!

Well, this made a real impression on David. He had been to the ocean hundreds of times. He vividly recalls those Saturdays as a boy when his dad would wake him up at 4 a.m. and announce, "We're going to the beach. Pack up your stuff and let's get moving!" His family would stop for breakfast on the way, arrive in Myrtle Beach later that morning, spend the day on the beach, find someplace to stay overnight, and get in a few more hours of beach time on Sunday before heading right home again. One spring and summer, David kept count—his family got away for mini-weekends to the beach like that 19 times! David's dad eventually bought a mobile home at the beach. Being down by the ocean was just a regular part of life.

Seeing that this was not always the case for other kids, David told his family that he wanted to create a non-profit to give others the kind of

Duryea Taylor and Gary chaperoning for KTTC

experience that he had always loved. With the Salvation Army Boys & Girls Club helping to select the kids and arranging for chaperones, Kids to the Coast became a reality, with David and his family forming a 501 (c) (3) and serving as Board members. In May 2018, Kids to the Coast completed its third trip to the ocean, with 26 more kids soaking up the sun and fun, along with ice cream at Painter's in North Myrtle Beach and everything else that will make the time memorable for them. Gary and Duryea Taylor served as drivers and entertained the kids with their many stories, and Diana from our office, who sits on the board of Kids to the Coast, helped out tremendously. In three years, Kids to the Coast has taken 52 kids to visit the beach, many for the first time. To learn more or to make a donation, visit www.kidstothecoast.org. A portion of the proceeds from the sale of this book will be donated directly to Kids to the Coast.

Finding ways to give back is a fundamental part of our faith and who we are. That's why we had to name "Honor GOD in all that we do" as our first core value for SMO. The other core values are:

We will SERVE our customers and team members.

In everything we do, we try to treat people the right way. We seek to be truthful and honest in our interactions and communication, and we hope to convey a sense of compassion and love toward those who entrust us with maintaining a healthy environment. We strive to serve our external customers by providing the most professional service possible, and we aim to serve our team members by respecting and appreciating who they are, not just what they do.

We will INNOVATE.

The cleaning services industry may not be on the cutting edge of technology, but we have done our best over the years to keep pace with or get out in front of the industry. We had car-mounted cell phones back around 1990, we always try to move quickly when new computer systems are introduced, and we made an early entry into the fast-growing realm of "green cleaning." After David read the pioneering book *Protecting the Built Environment: Cleaning for Health* by Michael Berry, Supreme Maintenance Organization branded its own approach to green cleaning. After cutting our teeth in the janitorial industry in the days when you had to regularly empty dozens of ashtrays and inhale toxic fumes, we applauded this new direction in choosing cleaning products and approaches that clean effectively without harming the environment. We understood that adopting green cleaning could improve the overall health and well-being of any operation, whether that's the bottom line of a business or attendance and test scores at a school. We have continued to enhance and refine our green cleaning program as it has become part of our standard operating procedures.

More recently, we have adopted a Corporate Sustainability program because we believe in a more sustainable, environmentally conscious and socially responsible future. As far as we know, very few of our competitors have taken this step. While the term "corporate sustainability" is relatively new, it's really something that was at the core of our beliefs back when we launched SMO in 1989.

We will CARE.

We subscribe to that saying that your customers don't care how much you know until they know how much you *care*. The proof is in the pudding—when you care, it will shine through in your work. This dedicated commitment is evident in the work our team members do every day. As we discussed earlier, we try to do our part to show our team members how much we care about them in everything from special awards and turkey giveaways to those little hand-written notes Gary writes on the back of outgoing mail and emergency loans we may provide when a team member faces an unexpected financial hardship.

We will act with INTEGRITY at all times.

Treating people the right way is part of acting with integrity. We're not boastful, but we'd like to think our behavior in whatever we do in operating SMO is above reproach. We have been told that for a multimillion-dollar business, we keep very clean books.

Acting with integrity, and all the other core values we commit to at SMO, are more than just business values to us. These are the values that guided our lives before they ever became our company's values.

While maintaining our core values, we also have sought to maintain clear roles within the organization so that our people understand our leadership structure and operation. As president, David oversees sales, finance, human resources, administration, and quality assurance. If there's a way to boil all that down, you could say that David's role is to make sure that our team members and our vendors all get paid, that receivables are collected, that we're not violating any laws, and the future of the business is being taken care of to the best of our ability. Around the office, we sometimes refer to David as the engine that drives our organization, or the rudder that keeps the ship steady.

David is the first to admit that Gary's got the tougher job because he's overseeing the people and operations out there on the frontlines of our cleaning services. Gary oversees three District Managers, who in turn oversee 12 Account Managers, who then direct hundreds and hundreds of Supervisors and Cleaning Technicians, who are really the foundation of it all.

So, when you look at the big picture, you find Gary with the ultimate responsibility for maintaining smooth operations and seeking continued improvement in how we serve our customers. To boil down Gary's role, you could say that he's got to keep our customers happy, he's got to keep our team members happy and he's got to keep David happy by continuing to keep accounts in budget.

Of course, each of us has his own personality and style. Gary is often lauded through the company ranks for his patience, while David admits he may not always be the *most* patient person around. David efficiently plows through his emails regularly throughout the day, while Gary may not always have time to open each email the moment it arrives. Gary is comfortable dealing face to face or by phone with many people day to day; David finds he is more productive operating primarily from inside the office.

We also turn to different outlets for managing the high-level stress that comes with running this kind of business. David keeps a salt-water aquarium in his office and pauses often to enjoy his connection with the water and to celebrate God's creation. Gary watches *The Price is Right* or *SportsCenter* on his flat screen TV or plays his favorite music—anything from old Southern rock to hip-hop to Christian to country—while in his office via Pandora. Gary also readily admits that when he takes a long drive, he is not one of those business executives who will use that time to listen to business or life enhancement books on CD. He'll stick with his tunes, thank you. We both still take our primary vacations at North Myrtle Beach, where we strive to stay unplugged.

Neither one of us is comfortable boasting about our positions as leaders of a successful business. In fact, when David is asked by strangers what he does for a living, he often says "I'm a janitor." If they push him on it, he may then add, "Well, I sit at a desk at a janitorial business all day now." Like our people, we try to stay humble.

Another thing the two of us share in common is the commitment to maintain a hands-on approach in the way that we've set up our organization and the manner in which we execute our roles. We both have our eyes and ears on the pulse of the business, and when major questions or problems arise, we will be right there to steer SMO through the troubled waters. In a way, we treat our business like one of our children. As a parent, at what age does your child become less important to you? We've both got kids in college or just out of college, and we still want to know as much as possible about what's happening with them. It's the same with SMO. It may be 30 years old now, with many more independent parts, but we still care about and want to know about everything that's happening in every domain. With our open-door policy, we sometimes field calls from our frontline staff. To make what we do work, we need to remain accessible.

As co-founders, we still communicate with one another all the time, sometimes for hours at a time, although we try to get home to our families before those midnight hours we used to keep when we were out cleaning together. We've both been involved in navigating all the changes our company has gone through over the years. As an example, hiring has evolved significantly as the business has expanded.

Hiring has always been a challenge for our business, both because of the pay range we can afford and the many different locations where our cleaning services are handled. When the economy is good, it's harder for us to attract job candidates. When the economy is bad, we get a lot more people lining up at our door. Of course, today they don't physically line up at our door because our applications are handled online. That's been one big change. We don't miss those days when we would run a newspaper ad over the weekend and on Monday morning the phone would be ringing off the hook. And you could never predict the response to any ad—sometimes it might pull in 100 applicants, sometimes it would be only a handful. Even with the challenges of hiring, we're proud to have been able to maintain turnover rates much lower than the industry norm. Unlike some others in our industry, we also steer away from under-the-table payment practices where someone is recruited to just clean a site for $250 a month but is never formally put on a payroll. Our people are employees and we take out taxes. That's part of operating with integrity.

So, guided by our faith and our core values, and steered by a clear organization with hands-on leaders, we have persevered through these 30 years and grown into a prominent regional business in the top three percent of our industry. But we're not done, not by a long shot. We take nothing for granted and realize it could all be gone tomorrow, but we have our sights set, God willing, on achieving a very specific goal for the future: $25 million in revenue by the year 2025.

Can we get there? If we maintain the average growth rate of 10-to-12 percent we've been able to achieve over the last 18 years, we believe we can achieve that goal. It's possible that one or more acquisitions may enter into the growth plan, and we'll make sure we have our eyes wide open to the impact of any change along those lines.

As we look into those possibilities for the future, and we acknowledge that neither of us is getting any younger, we recognize that there may come a day when this business that we have taken from a $200 start-up to a multimillion-dollar regional operation will be passed into the hands of somebody else. Will our family-oriented business stay in the family? Well, all our kids have worked at SMO in one capacity or another. It's going to be interesting to see if any of the Murphy or Collins kids decide to make their career at SMO. Diana jokes with us that as neat as it is for our people to say today that they're part of a company that's been around for 30 years, how much cooler will it be when someone can someday proclaim that as a team member of Supreme Maintenance Organization, they are a part of something that's been around for *a hundred* years?

Those are questions whose answers will only emerge over time. If we hold to our faith and our core values, hopefully it will all come out all right. Maybe more than all right!

CHAPTER 7

Lessons We Have Learned

W e've come a long way in 30 years. Starting with $200 and a borrowed vacuum cleaner as a couple of guys fresh out of college with no concrete plan, we somehow navigated a path to guide a successful regional business that provides work for more than 600 people and generates over $10 million a year in revenues. We've climbed toward the top of the cleaning industry. All this as co-founders of a company that one of us was sure would last six months, tops. (Gary still has to pinch himself to be reminded of the reality of where we are now, while David believes we have not yet reached our potential and holds onto that dream of someday flying in his own private jet!)

Along the way, we've weathered more storms than a sailor alone at sea, we've put or are putting our kids through college and we've managed to maintain and even strengthen a partnership that began when we were just middle school kids. I guess you could say we have figured out how to do a few things right, although we are the first to admit that we certainly have a lot more to learn and a long way to go to reach our goals in the cleaning industry.

We don't consider ourselves experts, and when we set out to put together this book we were very clear that we do not feel qualified to create any kind of how-to business success book. There are enough of those already out there anyway, right? But before we put away the mops and buckets, shut off the lights and lock up this operation, we thought we would highlight a few of the basic lessons we have learned over these 30 years. Maybe you'll find some of them useful, whether you happen to be joining this crazy world of cleaning services or have your sights set on leading a small business in another industry. The lessons are:

You don't have to be a straight-A student to build a successful business.

David likes to joke that if you added both of our high school GPA's together, the total would still be lower than the GPA of some of our kids. We certainly did not learn and practice the habits of hard work and dedicated effort in school. David never picked up a book and Gary was always trying to figure out what was the minimum you had to do to get by. Those are lessons we tried NOT to pass on to our kids and others we may be in a position to mentor.

David credits his wife, Paula, for the emphasis on academics in raising their four children. They even guided their kids into a Spanish immersion program so they are bi-lingual. Gary, in his role of coaching youth sports, tries to teach young people about what they need to do to succeed in life. He advises them that if the kid sitting next to them is not setting the bar high, they should ignore that influence and strive for excellence in their own lives. He also tells them not to fall into a pattern of only doing what you feel like doing because sometimes you have to do what is hard and necessary whether you feel like it or not. And he is also a believer in acting on your gut feeling because if you ignore your gut feeling and convictions long enough, they will go away and you will compromise your responsibilities, character and potential.

Fortunately, we have both been driven by a strive-for-excellence spirit in running our business. In the "classroom" of learning what is required to launch, grow and sustain a successful cleaning business, we have worked as hard as we could to stay afloat, get ahead and keep aiming higher. That's where we have been much better students—maybe still not straight-A students but solid achievers who maintain a clear focus and consistent effort.

One of the smartest things we have done was to join and fully utilize every opportunity for learning in the BSCAI, our primary trade association. The education, resources and networking through that forum have given us more than we ever imagined. Even now, when we attend a BSCAI event we come away with at least one nugget of information or some idea for a change in what we do that pays immediate dividends in our leadership with SMO. As an example, just a few years ago, we learned of the work opportunity tax credit that has saved our business thousands of dollars.

We have especially benefitted from the wisdom and experience of others who own cleaning companies through the Peer Group that we joined early on and remain committed to today. You heard from four of those group members earlier in the profiles of other successful cleaning businesses. As we mentioned, we take turns in the group visiting one another's companies, where the host business opens its books and all its operations so others can offer valuable input and suggestions for improvement. The experience can be humbling at times but always empowering.

So, if you are going to start or grow a cleaning business or comparable company, by all means join one or more trade associations. Go to their conventions and programs and commit yourself to coming away with at least one usable idea and a new, helpful contact every time. David still wonders if his father might have saved himself dozens of headaches and gone much further with his own janitorial company if he had gotten involved in trade associations.

Of course, when it comes to our "intelligence," we sometimes find that it can work to our advantage to point to our humble origins in the academic world. While we always act professionally, we often enjoy relating to customers in our region as a just a couple of good 'ole boys. Gary has been told by more than one customer, "You know, you're actually a lot smarter than you act." Gary replies with a laugh, "I'm pretty smart to be pretty dumb." Gary does know that you do not have to be very smart to understand that with the proper effort and attitude, you can achieve the desired results.

Another smart thing that any owner can do to succeed in the cleaning industry is to pick up the mop yourself. We started out doing all the cleaning ourselves, so our team members know that we understand what they go through. And sometimes when we bring on new mangers, we assign them an on-site cleaning task for a period of time so they also can appreciate the challenges that our Cleaning Technicians face on the frontlines. A key leadership trait is to lead by example and we all, at times, need to roll up our sleeves and pitch in to get the job done.

The bottom line is that if you didn't happen to waltz through school at the top of your class, you are in no way disqualified from major success in running a small business. You've just got to earn solid grades in the "classroom" of learning what to do to build your company, and you have to commit to the idea that nobody is going to study harder than you!

Treat every customer as if they are the biggest because someday they may be.

In the cleaning business, the competition is fierce. To achieve and sustain success, you have to accept the reality that even when you have landed a customer, it doesn't mean that your competitors will refrain from trying to lure that customer away from you and into their own clutches. That means you always need to make your customers feel that they are very important to you, as if they are the biggest or the only customer you have. If they call you on Saturday and inform you that they have a major visitor arriving Monday morning and need unscheduled top-to-bottom cleaning that weekend, you can't say, "Sorry, we can't do that." You've got to rise up to meet the challenge. And who knows, that special visitor coming in that Monday may lead to a major expansion for your customer—and a lot more business for you.

Around our office, we talk about how we need to turn our customers into raving fans, a term made popular in business through the Kenneth Blanchard book *Raving Fans: A Revolutionary Approach to Customer Service.* When Gary trains our managers, he uses the example of the wild and crazy Duke basketball fans who show up for big games in face paint and jump up and down from the opening tap to the final buzzer. (Being a Carolina alumnus, David is not real crazy about the Duke reference, but that's just life here on Tobacco Road.) While we don't expect our customers to suddenly start painting their faces, we can seek to maintain their passionate loyalty and trust by consistently performing at a high level in working for them. We try hard to build partnerships that last because as the old saying goes, it's easier to keep your customers than to get new ones.

As well as the benefit of holding onto your customers, treating each of them as if they are the biggest one really can result in them becoming your biggest customer. At SMO, it was our dedicated efforts in the early days of providing service for the Kmart DC and our current major logistics company that opened the door to much bigger accounts that elevated our business. We've also had many examples of satisfying a manager or executive at one company who then left and resurfaced at a much larger business. Because of our track record with that person, we earned this bigger account. So, if you enter into any agreement with a customer, no matter how small, invest in that relationship as if they matter the same as the customer that, for the moment, may be your biggest and most important one.

You earn your breaks.

We know that whatever success we've been able to achieve has come about because we have worked hard and just kept doing it. With our faith, we also might look at it as God allowing good things to come to us and our business because of how much effort we have shown and the faith that we maintain. Some may say that luck is involved, especially in a situation like we had with landing our first account with the Kmart DC just because we happened to have the right digits in our phone number. But the prefix of our phone number only got us in the door. We earned our way into a much bigger account through our hard work and dedication in serving that customer. You can't cheat business. It knows what you have invested and it won't give you anything you haven't earned.

Earning your breaks probably comes down to that spirit of perseverance that has kept our little engine chugging down the track. We've run into many obstacles and have been tested countless times along the way. In our first 10 years, we faced financial hardships that reached the point of worrying about whether we could make payroll. Sometimes we weren't able to pay ourselves on time so we could make sure that our employees received their paychecks.

Our philosophy has always been to take as little out of the company as we could in order to live reasonably comfortable lives. We don't own luxurious second properties in exotic locations. We don't give ourselves bonuses based on future profits, and we sure don't subscribe to the kind of wide income disparity everyone hears about between executives and front-line employees at many large companies and corporations these days. We're dedicated first and foremost to making sure we can sustain and grow our company, serve our customers and support our team members, and we believe it's that kind of dedication that has enabled us to be successful.

When we hear about folks who have visions of starting their own small business, we notice that many of them really don't understand what it takes. They think they can start a business, work 40 hours a week and sit back while the profits just naturally pour in. The truth is, when you start out you've got to have either money equity or sweat equity. We sure didn't have the money, so we knew we had to supply the sweat. Our willingness to work those long hours and make sacrifices at home, like not making it home for dinner or missing one of our kids' middle school graduations, helped to establish our reputation and attract more customers and bigger accounts. We really did earn our breaks, and that's the way we figure it works for most small business leaders in industries like ours.

Tomorrow you are one day closer to losing an account.

This is a simple lesson in reality. In the cleaning business especially, you're going to lose customers. It may be because of a change in owner-ship when your customer suddenly brings in their cousin or old friend to replace you. It may be because the customer has to put up the account for a national bid. It may be because some competitor drastically under-cuts your price. It may be your fault or it may be nobody's fault, but one way or another you will lose customers.

Complacency can be your enemy. Simply relying on previous success with a customer will not always guarantee loyalty. Many people know that you have to work hard to get what you want, but many fail to realize you have to also work hard to keep what you have. You really have to adopt a No Days Off mentality.

Once you accept the reality that you can't keep every one of your customers forever, you make two adjustments. First, you adopt that common business mindset that you're either growing or you're dying. In other words, you've got to keep recruiting and landing new accounts so you can more easily absorb the loss of one or more of your current customers here and there. Second, you remember that when ownership or management changes with one of your customers, the odds of losing that account rise and you must elevate your game to improve the odds of holding on to the account. That's when you invest even more time and energy into winning over the new boss because those relationships you had cultivated with the contacts you used to have there, no matter how solid they may have been, now mean nothing. You've got this "new customer" to impress.

Get the right people on the bus and put them in the right seat.

David learned this valuable business lesson from the excellent book *First, Break All the Rules: What the World's Greatest Managers Do Differently* by Marcus Buckingham and Curt Coffman. We've talked about how blessed we have been to attract people who have the right DNA to succeed in our business. In selecting team members for SMO, we sometimes use the reminder, "Don't *take* a cleaner, *make* a cleaner."

In other words, we don't care if a job applicant has experience in the cleaning industry. Often that can be a negative experience anyway. We care about them having the right character and the willingness to be led by that servant's heart we mentioned. You can teach them the technical skills or the management skills, but you can't teach their nature. You can't teach somebody to be responsible, to be dependable and to care. Recognizing that piece to the hiring equation is how you get the right people on the bus.

Now, when it comes to putting them in the right seat, we also learned that you can waste a lot of energy trying to fix people's weaknesses. It's far more productive to put them in a position where you take what they do well and provide them the opportunity to do more of that. As an example, after we had a better picture of Duryea "Juice" Taylor's energetic personality, we found that Quality Assurance Manager was a much more natural seat on the bus for him than being an Account Manager. That's how you support your people while also building a more productive and successful team.

Don't get distracted.

We've already admitted that for us anyway, investing a great deal of time and money into side ventures has, for the most part, really been a distraction that funneled some of the energy that could have been going into further growing and enhancing our company. Of course, many entrepreneurs have grown via new businesses and services, and it may work out that way for you. We would just urge caution and discretion when you are thinking about a new business venture that will take time away from your bread and butter.

We see many other examples of small business owners getting distracted. Usually it happens when they fall into an attitude that once they've begun to achieve even a small degree of success, they should be entitled to live a lavish lifestyle. Then they buy the three houses and a collection of expensive cars and they start turning up at all the most coveted places and major events, and all of a sudden, they're in way over their heads and piling up debts at a much faster rate than building any profit for their company. All of these material things are not inherently bad, but you cannot allow them to take priority over your core values or your business.

With our approach to growing a cleaning business, we work in a 7,000-square-foot office filled with second-hand or well-worn furnishings. Since we don't have to meet with customers in our office, we don't believe in wasting money that could be going into the company on flashy appearances where we do our work.

Another way that some owners get distracted is by getting caught in the false belief that you need to take every customer or account that may be available to you. For us, we needed to learn that it did not pay to clean retail operations. Our profits were going to come primarily from commercial cleaning, or businesses or organizations with several branches. Cleaning one retail store would divert valuable time and resources needed to achieve our goals.

Be very careful who you partner with.

Speaking from our experience, there is no bigger lesson to offer anyone choosing a similar path in business. Nothing that we have accomplished as a business would have been possible without the strength of our partnership. However, we tell people all the time not to enter into a business partnership lightly. When you choose someone else to work this closely with, you've got to establish and maintain a high level of trust. That's the foundation of any partnership.

For us, that trust began when we were best friends in high school, and

David and Gary have been partners for 30 years

it has only grown and deepened over time. But trust does not come just because you and a partner both want to get a business going and make it grow. It takes much more than a shared vision and a mutual desire for success. To create a successful partnership, you also need to share a personal connection that can't be broken. You need to have the same level of commitment and a similar work ethic. You need to be able to manage the differences and difficulties that will inevitably arise.

In our early years, we spent more time together than we spent with our wives. We had to navigate some rough spots, and we needed to build around our complementary personalities, skills and leadership styles. With us, it helped that David was a natural leader and Gary was an excellent follower. When two alpha personalities try to partner in a business, they usually clash.

Our faith has also served us in cultivating our partnership. When we face major decisions together, we pray that we will find a way to do what's best for our company and will leave each of us with a sense of peace about what we're deciding to do. We've been very fortunate that we've been able to keep doing that on the long road we've been following for 30 years.

If you are considering entering a business partnership, there is one more question that can provide a very valuable clue in whether it is right to move forward: Will this other person and his or her welfare and well-being always be more important to you than your company? That was true for us when we started this business with nothing, and it's still true for us in running a regional multimillion-dollar company today.

For us, the cleaning business is in our blood. Whoever you are, and whatever you may choose to do as you strive for excellence and success, we hope that you may experience the same kind of professional and personal fulfillment that we have been able to achieve, or something even greater. For us, we're just proud to say that over the course of 30 years, a couple of janitors have managed to create something worth honoring at this milestone moment as we have grown from rags to…more rags! Be Blessed and Bless Others!!!

Made in the USA
Middletown, DE
23 June 2024